Praise for the *Magic of M*

David Hodgson has, yet again, achieve... innovation and creativity. He has provided a simple process that can release immense creativity, curiosity and learning for both teachers and students. He reminds us not only about the importance and power of stories but also about how our own families can provide endless opportunities for learning and wonder if we took the time to ask the questions and listen to answers. I found myself strangely moved if not a little tearful. Magic.

Roy Leighton, educator, author and values consultant

Human beings cannot help but think of the world in terms of stories. The story amounts to an inbuilt template in our brains that puts our experience into context – remembering that 'context' and 'text' share the same root as 'textiles', meaning 'to weave'. Stories weave up the patterns of our lives. And both adults and children love to hear (and spin) a good yarn.

Stories are also powerful because they work at many levels. We can appreciate them for their beginning, middle and a satisfying resolution at the end. But the roots of story go deep into the symbolic, metaphoric and holistic realm of the subconscious mind; into the soil from which grows the sense we make of ourselves and the world we live in.

In the *Magic of Modern Metaphor* David Hodgson has assembled a treasure box of the most wonderful sparkling tales – light, accessible, humorous and elegant in their apparent simplicity; 'apparent' because like all good myths, legends and fairy tales they plant seeds in our psyches that in time will bear fruit in many delightful and surprising ways.

Steve Bowkett, author, storyteller, trainer

This book had me totally mesmerized from beginning to end! I found myself completely wrapped up in its spell as each little tale unfolded. The author takes us on a magical life-learning journey, using 'bite size' stories full of gentle humour and wisdom.

The metaphorical tales are genuinely heart-warming, without being sentimental, and all convey a spirit of hope and optimism.

David's unique approach to storytelling had me enthralled. The characters in the book seem to 'come alive' and it is easy for readers to relate to their various experiences – some funny, some inspirational and some very touching.

I can see this book being enjoyed by all ages and being used in a variety of different ways. As a professional therapist and trainer, I would certainly find the stories useful to use with clients, both adults and children alike. But I would take equal pleasure in sharing and discussing the tales with my own family.

In fact, the author himself makes some interesting and creative suggestions in the introduction, as to how the reader might approach the book and make use of this collection of learning tales.

I found this to be an extremely enjoyable, interesting and thought-provoking book, which reminded me of the effectiveness of metaphor and the incredible power of storytelling.

Michaela Gill, hypnotherapist

We all love stories as they are a vital part of our humanity passed on through the generations. These stories are a mixture of old and new and are written with compassion and humility. Many have an ethical base and offer opportunities for discussing the great challenges facing modern society. There are some nice touches of humour which children revel in and above all the stories are relevant to life and living today.

Dr David George, educational consultant

Magic of Modern Metaphor

Magic of Modern Metaphor

Walking with the Stars

Written and Illustrated by
David Hodgson
Edited by Nick Owen

Crown House Publishing Ltd
www.crownhouse.co.uk
www.crownhousepublishing.com

First published by
Crown House Publishing Ltd
Crown Buildings, Bancyfelin, Carmarthen, Wales, SA33 5ND, UK
www.crownhouse.co.uk
and
Crown House Publishing Company LLC
6 Trowbridge Drive, Suite 5, Bethel, CT 06801, USA
www.crownhousepublishing.com

British Library of Cataloguing-in-Publication Data
A catalogue entry for this book is available
from the British Library.

10-digit ISBN 184590394-3
13-digit ISBN 978-184590394-7
LCCN 2009936674

Printed and bound in the UK by
The Cromwell Press Group,
Trowbridge, Wiltshire

Dedicated to Jonty, Terry and Grandads everywhere
for the magic they make.

Foreword

A storyteller was once challenged to justify the value of stories. 'What contribution could they possibly make,' he was asked, 'to individuals, society and civilisation?'

The storyteller said: 'Let me tell you a story ...

Once upon a time three travellers were crossing the great wilderness of NOW on horseback. After a few years, they'd settled into some sort of routine. Each night, after a hard day's journeying, they would unsaddle their horses, unpack their saddlebags, pitch their tents, eat dinner, check their e-mail and go to bed.

One night, just before bedtime, they were surprised to see a glimmer of light on the horizon. It grew stronger and stronger until its brilliance filled the whole of the night sky. And each traveller intuitively knew he or she was in the presence of some kind of Divine Being, and each one waited for the words of God that they knew were bound to come.

And the words came, and the words said: 'Go forth into the wilderness. Gather as many pebbles as you may, and tomorrow will find you surprised, delighted, disappointed, and very ... very ... curious.'

And that was it. End of message. The last echoes of the deep and rumbling voice faded and the light dimmed and died. And the travellers stood there in the silent darkness. Until one exploded in frustration, 'What kind of a God was that? Gather pebbles! The uselessness of it! We're respectable travellers not pebble collectors. We want meaning and purpose in our lives.'

The second traveller added, 'A real, value-for-money God would have offered us something practical and tangible. You know, how to get rich or be successful. What's the point of pebbles?'

The third traveller said, 'Divinely inspired wisdom would have showed us how to cut carbon emissions and other ways to save the planet. How on earth can pebble collecting be a sustainable and rewarding activity?'

But perhaps because of the gravitas of the voice and the force of the Messenger's delivery, the three travellers did hunt around for a short time, gathered a few pebbles each and threw them dismissively into the depths of their saddlebags. And then they went to bed.

In the morning they rose, packed up, saddled up and rode off towards their distant and dimly perceived destination. And after another day's travelling they went through their usual evening routine. Then, just before dinner, one went to fetch something he needed from the bottom of his saddlebag. And as he rummaged for it, his hand happened on something small, round and hard. Of course, a pebble!

But when he pulled it out and discovered it was a diamond, you might imagine how surprised he was. And he called his companions over. And they too discovered that all their pebbles had become diamonds. And you can imagine how delighted they were.

Until they considered how few, in their disdain and delusion, they had collected. And you may imagine how disappointed they were.

But as they were drinking their espressos and malted lattes around the campfire after dinner, they got to enquiring into the meaning of all this. The small pieces of rock which the previous night they had considered so worthless were now precious. And they began to wonder how many other things in their lives, things that they had previously considered of little or no consequence, might have a value that they hadn't discovered, considered or even dreamed of yet.

And they began to get more and more curious about discovering meanings under the surface of things, which only now were they beginning dimly to comprehend with growing excitement and wonder.

David Hodgson is just like this storyteller. Through story, metaphor, anecdote and the ebb and flow of relationships and understandings, he points us gently and with great compassion towards making our own discoveries about the value of life and experience, and some of the great questions that challenge our society and civilisation today.

In the *Magic of Modern Metaphor: Walking with the Stars,* David offers countless pebbles of wisdom for each of us to consider, reflect upon and explore for the depths of their meaning and the knots of relevance hidden under the surface of his stories and their quirky, entertaining, episodic narratives.

The themes he explores are critical if we are to provide stability and firm foundations for the sustainable development of ourselves and our societies in the years to come: these themes include family, community, continuity, tradition, sacrifice, expertise and ethics. The themes are as unfashionable as they are absolutely essential, if we are to survive this current depressing and self-referential era of rampant individualism, political correctness and one-size-fits-all-ism. Yet David has the skill and finesse to put these themes across with a delightful lightness and elegance that connects with our innate humanity and common sense, whatever our age, experience or background.

My prediction is that David's stories will *surprise* you with their charm, variety and self-honesty.

They will *delight* you with their humanity and vitality, their nostalgia, insight, wit, wisdom and relevance.

You may even find yourself *disappointed* to discover, once you've made your acquaintance with the wonderfully eclectic collection of human beings, animals, birds, creatures and ghostly apparitions that inhabit these pages, that there aren't more stories on offer.

And you will surely be *curious* to explore for yourself not only the hidden meanings and applications beneath the surface of these stories, but also the way they may elicit resonant memories from your own life; memories whose significance and relevance to your own learning and development still awaits your fully focused attention and interpretation.

This book has found you. Now it is for you to find out why.

Nick Owen
Editor, storyteller and leadership mentor

Acknowledgements

Thank you to everyone at Crown House Publishing for their support and to Nick Owen, now an honorary Northerner.

Acknowledgments

Contents

Part III: Interpreting the Stories   **141**

Part I
Introducing the Stories

'We were making the future,' he said, 'and hardly any of us troubled to think what future we were making. And here it is!'

The Sleeper Awakes, *H. G. Wells*

Angel of the North

Introduction

The *Angel of the North*

On an exposed windy hillside in Gateshead an individual stands confidently over a community. When erected in 1998 the *Angel* divided local opinion; awe on one side and 'couldn't a million pounds be better spent?' on the other.

The *Angel* has stood for over ten years now and it makes a difference. Once something exists it can't not make a difference. It is part of the landscape but still seems to float above it. It can inspire and surprise each time you see it. I have driven by it many times on my way to a work event or on a family outing and its power is palpable. In my little bubble, in my little car, with my little worries I've caught a glimpse of the sun on a wing or the mighty silhouette against a huge tarmac grey sky and I'm taken out of my bubble, if only for a moment. A moment is long enough to contemplate better questions.

The *Angel* represents an investment in art and imagination over the practical and 'real'. When combined, these two become a powerful force. Although the initial million pound price tag seemed excessive to many, an original bronze maquette (model) owned by Gateshead Council was valued at one million pounds on an episode of *Antiques Roadshow*, the highest valuation given to any object in the history of the programme. The true value of things is not always obvious. Time changes and places change and so can people, individually and as communities. People often feel threatened by change. Yet only when we change do we grow and develop.

The *Angel* changes slowly. Its rusty colour is mellowing with age. It was built to last for a hundred years. Soon after its installation, the *Angel* was adorned with a huge black and white striped football shirt bearing the name 'Shearer' and the number 9, though only for twenty minutes until police arrived to remove it. The names of future North-Eastern heroes are as yet unknown but the *Angel* will be there as their stories unfold.

When Antony Gormley is asked to explain his *Angel of the North* he offers three thoughts: to remember the generations of coal-miners who worked in the darkness beneath the hill for two hundred years, to highlight the change from the industrial age to the information age and as a focus for us to explore our hopes and fears.

Gormley's overall theme of a community seeking an identity through changing times resonates with everyone at an individual level. As we grow up we search for our own identity within our community, and this collection of stories reflects our individual journeys.

As we immerse ourselves in information, as a species, we could do well to remember that our own senses bombard us with perhaps three million pieces of information per minute. As individuals we filter and use only a small amount of this information. Understanding this filtering process and using it wisely is more useful than gorging on information.

Occupational psychologists studying human performance have explored the impact of training in four areas: information, skills, attitude and habits. Their research suggests that business generally concentrates on information and skills when it is attitude and habits that have a greater long-term impact on performance. Although attitude and habits are more difficult to influence, stories can offer a gentle yet profound route to challenge and change them.

Education, too, has increasingly focused on squeezing information and skills into a crowded curriculum. Perhaps we should remember that schools were originally formed in Ancient Greece to allow students and teachers the opportunity to share their ideas and perceptions. Such a two-way process grows attitude and habits. The word education derives from the Latin *educare* meaning 'to draw out'. We are not blank slates, and stories are a rewarding method for drawing out the wisdom within all of us.

The majority of our attitudes and habits are formed as we grow up. If we are lucky children we are surrounded by angels influencing us in positive ways. Siblings, peers, parents, teachers, neighbours and communities are benign or malevolent guides. Grandparents, at their best, are the most powerful angels of all because their influence can spread through time, acting as a bridge linking the generations.

When we interpret stories we can't be wrong. We create meaning that is right for us in that time and place. The stories presented in this collection offer the reader an opportunity to explore their attitudes and habits. Once we are able to gain greater clarity in these areas we can better develop our knowledge and hone our skills to be effective individuals and valuable members of our communities.

Ten methods for getting the most out of this book

Stories are the most important thing in the world. Without stories, we wouldn't be human at all.

Philip Pullman

I'd like to encourage you to write your thoughts on the pages of the book itself (unless you're in a bookshop as this can annoy staff). This is a great way to personalise the stories.

And if you do turn out to be famous, the scribbles you make in this book could make it far more valuable to wealthy collectors in the future. However, any financial benefits will probably be enjoyed by your children or grandchildren some time after you're gone.

A psychologist studied two Native American tribes that lived side by side. One tribe allowed their infants to crawl freely and the other tribe restricted their movements. The tribe that allowed their children freedom were more advanced in terms of arts and crafts, tools used, writing and performing as a group. When we interact with our environment we learn more. I recommend you interact with the stories that follow.

Method 1

Relax. Read a few stories and stop when you find something particularly interesting. Reflect.

On a piece of paper write down five thoughts that occur to you. They could include: the meanings of the story, personal memories, how the story relates to things currently going on in your life or anything else. Return to your thoughts later.

Method 2

Read two stories (random or consecutive) and think of a way to link them.

Method 3

Read a story and ask yourself: How can I apply this in my own life?

Method 4

Read a story and ask yourself: What would I do next?

Method 5

Identify someone you admire and read a story as if you were that person. Then ask yourself what they would think of the story.

Method 6

Ask yourself: How would I change or improve a story?

Method 7

Ask yourself: What are my memories from childhood (people and/ or events)?

Method 8

Roll a dice and then summarise the story in that number of words.

Method 9

Ask yourself: With whom would I like to walk? Next time you go on a walk imagine they are with you. Have a conversation (but best to do it inside your head unless it is a secluded walk).

Method 10: The group method

It's not just good to share your sweets. Discuss the stories with a friend or group of friends if you're lucky enough to have more than one. There is a great deal of research confirming the benefits of sharing our thoughts, ideas, opinions and dreams.

Part II
The Stories

If the doors of perception were cleansed everything would appear to man as it is, infinite.

William Blake

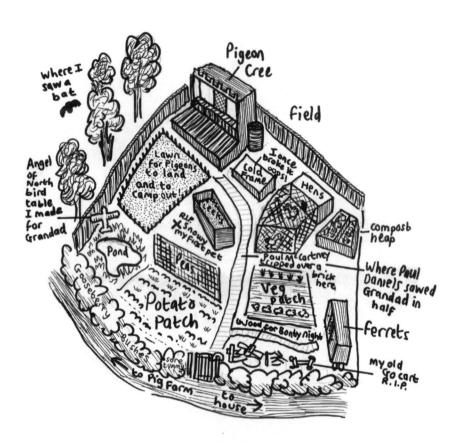

Pigeon Cree

Field

Where I saw a bat

Angel of North bird table I made for Grandad

Lawn for Pigeons to land and to Camp out!

I once broke it oops!

Cold Frame

Hens

Compost heap

R.I.P. Snowy my first pet

Pond

Peas

Paul M'Cartney tripped over a brick here

Where Paul Daniels sawed Grandad in half

Gooseberry

Potato Patch

Veg Patch

Wood for Bonty night

Ferrets

Bushes

sore tummy

to Pig Farm

to house →

my old Go cart R.I.P.

1. *Swapping allotments*

While digging some compost into the area where potatoes would be planted later in the year, Jack asked Grandad how it was that he had the best allotment. It certainly seemed to be the biggest and best, for it was situated at the end of the row bordered by a field, a hedgerow of gooseberries and a small wooded area.

'Well, I went to see the bloke who had it before me, Mr Jenkins. I spoke to him for a while. He seemed to be the kind of person that liked to concentrate on the things he didn't have rather than the things he did have.'

'What do you mean?'

'He told me the soil was too dry on the slope at the back. There was too much shade from the trees over there. It was the allotment furthest away from the village so it was a longer walk to reach it. I can't remember the other things but there were many. I told him all the things I'd done to my previous allotment and that I'd basically finished making it the best it could be. So we agreed to swap.'

'And you've made this allotment as good as it can be Grandad, haven't you?'

'Yes, and he went and made my old allotment as bad as it could be.'

2. *Birds that flock together learn together*

While walking to the allotment Jack asked Grandad why he still had milk delivered to the door when it was cheaper to buy it at the shops. Grandad said there were a few reasons.

'Firstly, habit. We've always had milk delivered to the house and so did our parents before us. I also remember my Dad saying when they had milk delivered before the war the bottles didn't have lids. Blue tits and robins learned to sit on the rim and drink the cream that settled at the top of the bottles. Years later foil lids were introduced and for a while all the birds were denied this easy and regular meal. Then the blue tits learned to tap away at the foil to break a hole in it and they could feed again. The robins did not learn this new skill.

'Now, I've watched these birds and I've noticed that tits are sociable. They spend a lot of time in family and extended groups. Robins are more territorial and aggressive. They like their own space, thinking that if they can feed in a large area on their own they'll have more food. Over the last few decades tits have done well and robin numbers have declined. Birds that flock together learn together, passing on their learning for the whole group to benefit.

'We get milk delivered because I know the milkman and his family. We live in a community here, Jack, and I think we're all better for it.'

3. *Who is your favourite?*

Jack had convinced himself that his sister Rosy was the favourite. On his way to help his grandad feed the pigeons he had gathered an impressive list of evidence to present to him. He had five pieces of proof. Three examples are usually enough, even one. His grandad listened as Jack posed his question: 'Why do people like Rosy better than me?'

Grandad considered while scooping equal amounts of feed into two tins for Jack and himself to distribute to the pigeons, Jack to the pigeons on the left and Grandad to the right of the battered clock hanging in the middle of the cree. He asked Jack to complete the job they had both done many times.

Grandad asked Jack if he already knew the answer to his question. Jack nodded enthusiastically and offered to share his five examples. 'No need,' said Grandad as they watched the birds jostle for position to take their share of feed. Puffs of agitated dust from the birds and their feed floated up and mixed with the dry August air.

Grandad asked Jack for five things he liked about winter at the allotment. It didn't take long for Jack to come up with them: catching snowflakes as they fell from the sky onto his outstretched tongue; watching huge icicles grow from the cree roof ledge like stalactites that glistened in the sunlight, and their cold, smooth, alien texture and taste on dry winter days; holding the heavy icicles in his hand until he numbed his fingers through the cold; walking carefully on the small, slippery, iced-over pond and hoping to hear a crack and snap followed by the white jagged lines rushing and branching out from under his shoes like bolts of lightning; and making snowmen that looked like members of his family.

Grandad asked Jack for five things he liked about summer at the allotment and Jack complied and compiled: staying out longer because it's warm and doesn't get dark till late; ice creams when it's hot and dry; listening to the cricket on the little radio and playing cricket by the leek trench; chasing escaped hens around the allotment and getting them back into their pen; and building dens in the hedge.

Grandad asked, 'First, did you notice how easy it is to think of five reasons you like or dislike something?' Jack nodded.

'Second, that different questions about the same subject can generate different answers? Asking what you like about two different things produces different thoughts and answers to questions using the word *best*.'

'And which gives the best answer?' asked Jack.

'Think "most useful" answer rather than "best" answer. If I'd asked for your favourite season you would have had five ideas but because I asked what you liked about two seasons you had ten ideas. I like to remember that there are many questions and many answers but most tell us nothing that is real or useful. Many make us unhappy if we forget they are just thoughts. They provide us with information but not knowledge.

'Let me give you an example. I can remember the second thing on your list of things you like about summer, and here is some money for you to go to the shop now to buy an ice cream. There's enough money for you to buy one for me too.'

'What kind of ice cream would you like, Grandad?'

'That's the most useful question you've asked me today.'

Grandad's
favourite
pigeon

4. *Blowing up balloons*

It was Aunt Joy's birthday. Jack came in from playing football and sat next to Grandad. All of the adults were blowing up balloons in preparation for the birthday party. Birthdays were basically the same as a normal Sunday tea but with balloons and a birthday cake with candles replacing pontoon and apple pie with custard. Jack noticed parties for very old people were very similar to parties for very young people.

Uncle Bill threw a few balloons at Jack as an invitation to contribute to the party preparations. He thought it was funny watching the adults gasp and wheeze for breath as their faces and necks turned darker shades of beetroot.

He asked his grandad why the straight ones were harder to blow up than the pear-shaped balloons. 'That's a good question, Jack. I don't know the answer but sometimes a good question is useful without a good answer.' Jack then noticed Grandad was the only person blowing up only round balloons. He winked at Jack and threw him a couple of round balloons. Aunt Joy looked so purple Jack thought she might not live long enough to blow out the candles on her birthday cake.

5. *Paper knickers*

Aunt Joy's eighty-third birthday passed by smoothly. Jack was pleased with his contribution which amounted to three balloons and an invitation to his Aunt to reminisce about the paper pants purchased for a family camping holiday to Crimdon Dene. After the celebrations Jack and his grandad were desperate to escape the stifling living room. Grandad once said it shouldn't be called the living room as there was little sign of any life. He often said, 'You're either living or you're dying, which are you doing?'

After a suitably lengthy pause in conversation Grandad used a suspected ferret pregnancy as his excuse to escape to the allotment. The last straw had been Aunt Joy saying just after she'd blown out the candles that it might be the last time she ever did it. She was good at blowing out some things.

At least Aunt Joy didn't spend her birthday with her cousin's catalogue on her lap. She spent at least an hour every Sunday flicking through the catalogue and to this day she had never once bought anything. The familiar flick of the thin pages and her exaggerated lick of her finger to create full purchase on the page for turning were part of a familiar rhythm of sounds Jack associated with the house. She occasionally commented on the content, with '£5 for a cardigan!' accompanied by a tut and shake of the head that the elderly specialise in, or 'isn't that woman ugly – she should be modelling the hooded coats not the lingerie' or 'that lass has thighs like a rugby player not an underwear model', delivered with deadpan disgust and dismay.

On the way to the allotment Jack asked why Aunt Joy was so miserable. He asked Grandad why her memories of family holidays were always of the bad things that had happened whereas everyone else remembered the funny things. Every family has funny stories that result in tears of laughter all round. The paper knickers purchased for a camping holiday was one such family story in the Star household. Perhaps a good idea at the time but in a wet campsite they provided little of the necessary warmth and protection needed for a camping holiday in the North-East. Jack had experienced local beaches during unforgiving biting gales. The scant respite of an ice cream, coated in sand which whipped horizontally across the shoreline, was the day's only reward. Even raspberry sauce can't make a mouthful of scaly, salty sand tasty.

Jack had offered Aunt Joy the chance to enjoy the paper pants anecdote and she chose to complain about her parents and their poor choice of holidays, citing the knickers as the probable cause of some of her many ailments and illnesses.

'Yes, Jack, I had noticed,' said Grandad. 'What do you choose to remember?'

'Both, I suppose. The good and the bad.'

'Well that's OK when you're eleven.'

'I'm twelve, Grandad.'

6. *A sting*

Jack excitedly shared information about wasps that he'd learned in a wildlife documentary that week. The wasp injects a fat pupa with its eggs and then paralyses it to keep it fresh and alive so its own larvae have a good source of food. The host is slowly eaten alive from the inside, unable to move. Jack thought this was a horrible and cruel way to die.

Later, Jack was taking some clippings over to the compost heap in the wheelbarrow and spotted a dead animal in the hedge. Intrigued, he settled the barrow and closed in on the carcass to investigate. It was a bird, a blackbird he thought, that had been dead for some time. By a clump of young nettles he saw a stick. As he picked it up he brushed against the nettles and stung himself. He initially ignored the stings on his hand as he used the stick to flip over the fading body. As he did so a few fat, creamy-white maggots started to wriggle through the empty eye socket. Grandad had noticed Jack take an unscheduled break and was now standing at his side.

'Urggh,' sighed Jack. 'Why are some animals so disgusting?'

'Well, I'd be careful which animals you dismiss. Those maggots help to make sure there aren't dead animals all over the place. And, in the army, maggots were used to keep wounds clean because they only eat dead flesh.'

Jack saw the raised skin on his hand and felt the itchy sting of the nettle take effect.

'Well, what about nettles? They're annoying.'

'Only when they sting you. They make a delicious soup. They were also used for thousands of years across Europe to make fishing nets and cloth. The Germans used nettles instead of cotton during the war to make clothes. I think your Aunt Joy has knickers made out of nettles which would explain the look she wears on her face. Nettles could be used in the future as an environmentally friendly crop, who knows. It is often in the most surprising times and places that you find the most useful answers. Now let's find some dock leaves for that sting.'

7. Dragonfly, frogs and toads

Jack asked Grandad if he'd been popular at school. Grandad enquired why he asked, which he often did, and Jack said a new boy had joined his school and he wasn't popular. First he had tried to get in with the tough kids but they weren't interested. Then he tried to be friends with the boys who play football but because he wasn't very good they didn't let him play.

'Do you know why I built that little pond down there?'

'No.'

'Let me show you. It means less room for potatoes but more room for loads of animals.'

He led Jack quietly down through the ferns and horsetails that grew between the pond and the hedge and told Jack he didn't understand why the term 'pond life' was used to describe bad people because pond life was amazing. They knelt down as Grandad pointed out different creatures that scurried about in and around the pond. Jack was reminded of the time when they sat almost hypnotised when a dragonfly hovered and then rested briefly on a horsetail stalk. Its neon blue body shone so brightly in the sunlight that it took their breath away.

'Look at all those little creatures, Jack. They all find their place. Some live only on the surface – that one there is called a water boatman. Others live just below the surface and some tucked away out of sight. We all have to find our place. Some stand out, like the dragonfly we saw. Others are hardly noticed but they're all important.

The main thing is to find the place best suited to you. Remember not to ignore other creatures. They could surprise you and help you.'

'Which do you like best, Grandad?'

Jack knew his grandad liked frogs and toads. Jack had seen frogs around the pond in the hedgerow at the bottom of the allotment and a few toads at the top of the garden by the pots next to the greenhouse wall. His grandad liked to share his enthusiasm for toads and frogs.

He explained: 'Toads get a bad press because they're warty and people think this means they're dirty creatures that spread disease. They're actually very tame and clean. So tame that toads were used in the olden days when people travelled around the country selling potions that could cure all kinds of illness. The seller would ask a man in the crowd to swallow a toad and then offer him the special potion to survive. This man would secretly be working for the seller and was known as a *toady*, which is where the expression originates.

'Frogs too are amazing animals. Some secrete poison from their skin that can kill a man. Another frog wraps its eggs in a sort of foam that protect them from attack by weather and bacteria. Scientists have identified the chemical and are exploring ways to use it to protect wounds and repair and heal skin. Frogs may hold the secret to curing many diseases, such is their variety. We must be careful about judging people as well as animals, Jack, because until you find out you can't really know what they're like. It's not really about being popular or not; it's better to get to know what's good about someone and what you have in common.'

8. *Gandhi visits the allotment*

While potting on some cabbage seedlings into larger pots, Grandad started to tell Jack about the time Gandhi came to the allotment. He'd been to the house first for tea. Aunt Joy had taken a shine to him. Only the second bloke she'd ever smiled at while looking him in the eyes. The first, a welder from Consett, was so frightened he moved abroad.

'Aye, canny fella that Gandhi. He helped me pot on some cabbages. He sat just where you're sitting, Jack. After we'd finished he insisted we arm-wrestle. He was a great arm-wrestler for a little bloke. I made a negative comment about Joy and Gandhi seemed to be fascinated by that. He then said I was part of a big family and that's a good thing. He predicted that families would become smaller around the world and it would pose the biggest threat to mankind. He thought we all needed to bear in mind that we're better when we remember we're part of a big family.'

9. Barking (1)

Grandad sometimes collected Jack and Rosy from school and took them for a walk before going home. There was a wood near the allotments and Grandad would make sure the walk was interesting by sharing some of the secrets of the wood – mostly about ghosts. They would sometimes pass a house with a high fence and a dog would bark loudly as they walked past. Grandad reassured Rosy, who flinched sometimes when the first bark interrupted their journey.

'Some people are like the barking dog. They are aggressive and rude to just about everyone. The dog doesn't know who it's barking at and neither do some people. After a time these people forget who or what they're barking at but we learn to keep out of their way. This is one way people protect themselves from the attentions of others. If that dog found a gap in the fence it could distinguish between friendly and unfriendly people. It would know we're friendly and we might even bring it treats like we do for the one-eyed horse.'

10. Barking (2)

Another time Grandad, Jack and Rosy passed the house and the dog barked so aggressively that all three jumped, fearing the dog might burst out from somewhere along the fence and attack.

Grandad remarked that we all have two dogs inside of us battling for supremacy. One is cold, angry, nervous, jealous and negative, like the dog on the other side of the fence. The other is warm, friendly, loving and hopeful, the kind of dog that is excited to see you, wagging its tail and licking your face. We forgive its horrid breath because it is great to be around.

Jack asked, 'Which dog wins the battle?'

His grandad replied, 'Whichever one you feed the most.'

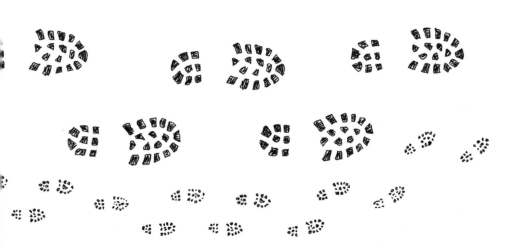

11. *Gooseberry fools*

Jack and Rosy were walking up to the allotment. Grandad had sent them to the shop to buy an ice cream while he repainted the pigeon cree. Rosy asked Jack if he'd ever been told off by Grandad. They discovered that neither of them could remember ever being scolded by Grandad.

Then they remembered the time they'd asked Grandad if the gooseberries were ripe on the huge hedge that stretched along the bottom perimeter of most of the allotment. They were told to wait until the following week. They'd ignored the advice and proceeded to greedily demolish the whole crop like a swarm of hungry locusts. What they didn't eat became weapons to hurl at each other. Some of the gooseberries were so sour they could hardly be chewed. They laughed as they watched each other's faces twist and contort in agony as the berries burst inside their mouths releasing a package of sloppy seeds in an acidic explosion. Crunching through the greener berries was a challenge they were both up to. Relief was temporary when a sweet, ripe berry burst onto the tongue. Sometimes they would spit out a sour berry impersonating Bob Carolgees's Spit the Dog.[1]

When they returned to the allotment they asked Grandad why he hadn't got upset following the gooseberry incident. He revealed that he clearly remembered the episode as he had watched from the hill just above the allotment while waiting for returning pigeons. He said it was one of the funniest things he'd seen and he knew that punishment would be delivered by the berries themselves. He was right because both Jack and Rosy had a terrible tummy ache that evening and hadn't been able to eat a gooseberry since.

---

[1] Man and puppet double acts have always been popular on British TV. In the 1970s Spit the Dog, although a one trick pony (he spat), enjoyed a fairly lengthy period of fame. Spit was Liam to Bob's Noel. Rod Hull and Emu were the 'A' list act, though their crown was nearly stolen by Keith Harris and Orville who branched into novelty records while Mr. Blobby was still in Nappies. Modern day equivalents, such as Philip Schofield and Gordon the Gopher and Ed and Oucho, are consigned to minor slots on TV because Ant and Dec occupy most prime-time Saturday night shows. Neither Ant nor Dec are glove puppets.

12. *Inside out*

Grandad had noticed Jack being nicer to his sister than normal and asked why. Jack confessed that Rosy had been feeling down this week because some girls at school had said she wasn't as pretty as they were. Grandad said he'd got two new animals at the allotment and if Jack and Rosy could guess what they were on the way to the allotment they could name them.

Jack ran up to the allotment ahead of Grandad and Rosy so he could see the new animals first. Grandad had two new hens and they were worth seeing. Their feathers shone a bright golden and black colour in the afternoon sun. The birds scratched around their pen looking for any grain they had missed earlier. When Grandad and Rosy caught up, Grandad asked what they thought and both children said they were amazed. Rosy asked if their eggs would taste better than those of the plain hens. Grandad said he doubted it but they would find out soon enough.

He added: 'Birds really are beautiful animals. So many species have beautiful plumage. Their colours, shapes and movement can take your breath away. On top of that many sing really well too. Not many species look or sound as good as birds to us humans. Do remember, though, pluck away the feathers and they'd all look pretty much the same. Like humans, birds pay far too much attention to what they look like. What's inside is far more important.'

Rosy didn't seem to be paying attention so Grandad asked Jack to fetch some feed for the hens while he showed Rosy a buddleia tree he'd also brought in this week. He showed Rosy the tree and explained how important it was to ensure the roots were well placed and gently firmed in. He explained that the tree would grow well here and provide shade for the hens once it grew and attracted insects and worms. He suggested that if you judged the tree now you'd say it wasn't very good. But the tree would grow quickly and if it were evaluated next year it would be judged favourably. As long as it was cared for it would thrive. He said Rosy was similar. If people judged her now it was silly. She would grow and change – as long as her roots were strong. He also said he was there to care for not only the buddleia.

13. *Outside in*

Next week Grandad wanted to show Rosy the leeks. He was more excited than she was but Rosy humoured him.

'Look, I've named them all after supermodels, Rosy. Don't you think they look like supermodels, long, straight and in their own catwalk? Some of my leeks might weigh more than supermodels though. We could put some of your old dolls' clothes on these and it would be like a catwalk show in Milan or Paris.' They spent a few minutes going through the names of each leek.

'Which leek do you think will taste the best?'

'I don't know,' said Rosy, but then she pointed at the one they'd named Twiggy.

'You might be right there. But you can't really know until you cook them. Now I'm not suggesting we eat supermodels, but what's inside is more important than looking just at the outside. People get this inside out. You won't, will you, Rosy? You'll not judge people or leeks by how they look?'

'No.'

'I'm glad because I used to be a supermodel, you know. I used to model wellies at the Miners' Gala.'

14. Hairstyle

Jack asked Grandad what Aunt Joy had meant when she said Grandad was 'too positive'. She'd said if he woke up bald he'd probably look in the mirror and think, that's great I don't have to go to the barber's any more.

'Well, I suppose compared to Aunt Joy I could look very positive. Next time she says that, tell her that if I had only one hair I'd be pleased because I could have a ponytail. If I had two hairs I'd still be pleased because I could have a parting. If I had three hairs I'd be pleased because I could have my first plait.'

Jack suggested that if he had four hairs he could copy Aunt Joy's hairstyle. They laughed as they both pulled faces to impersonate Aunt Joy.

15. *Walking with Freddie Mercury*

On a crisp autumn day the walk to the wood had slowed to a snail's pace because Rosy said she was tired. She'd been singing Queen's 'Another One Bites the Dust' so Grandad said he'd invited Freddie Mercury to join them on their walk.

'He should be waiting for us at the corner of this field. What do you think he'll be wearing Rosy?'

'Well, it's a bit cold so I hope he's not wearing a skin-tight Lycra out-fit,' reasoned Rosy. 'And there are nettles and brambles on the way.'

'If he is you might have to let him borrow your parka, Jack,' continued Grandad.

As they approached the corner Grandad suggested they listen carefully as Freddie might be singing. Grandad said he thought he could see Freddie walking ahead. Their pace quickened and the children moved in front.

'Should we follow him to see where he's going?' asked Grandad. Before he'd heard a reply Grandad bustled his way past the children and headed off through the ferns away from the main path. The smell of wild garlic intensified as they followed a smaller path that wriggled its way between the mature trees. Their leaves flickered in the breeze but it was the sound of feet trampling over clumps of grass, snapping dry rotten branches and squelching through damp ditches that spread through the woodland.

'Where is Freddie heading for, Grandad?' asked Jack.

'I think he's heading for the conker trees.'

A few minutes later they reached the conker trees. The children had been here last year with Jimmy Savile[2] so they knew what to do. They scoured the ground looking for prickly conker shells. They found many and enjoyed tearing them apart, revealing soft new conkers. Grandad had told the children that when they opened a fruit to remember they were the first person to ever see the conker inside. It

---

[2] Imagine a cross between Chris Moyles and Ali G.

had taken months for it to grow from a tiny dot. They enjoyed this thought every time they discovered a conker shell. You could never predict a good conker from the state of the fruit. Some unpromising fruits produced magnificent plump conkers with skins as beautiful as dark-wood antique furniture. They stuffed their pockets with conkers. They would examine and sort them later from the warmth of home. They would not have to force any fruit down from the trees as there were so many on the woodland floor.

Grandad said he'd thought Freddie would have got all these conkers but he mustn't have anywhere to store them. He told the children that Freddie was a good conker player but not as good as Jimmy Savile. Grandad suspected Savile cheated but, as he couldn't be sure, he suggested the children just remember to put their money on Savile if they're ever asked to bet at a celebrity conker tournament. The children committed this advice to memory.

'The last time I was with Freddie he was telling me about a masked ball he'd attended. There were loads of celebrities there. He said you couldn't tell who was who because the disguises were so good. He said it was the best party he'd ever been to because you could be whatever personality you wanted to be. The mask gave you amazing confidence. It gave you the chance to be your best or worse. It seems strange to think that celebrities aren't confident but in my experience most of them don't know who they are. Freddie said in normal life it's the other way round. People wear a mask which covers their underlying confidence and courage. It stops most people being the person they could be. At this party the masks allowed everyone the freedom to experience fully and not fear mistakes. The conkers have a mask too. It's great to see what's inside the fruit. I'm looking forward to seeing what's inside both of you.'

16. *Too small to make a difference*

'Grandad, you're always telling us we are important but can one person really make a difference?'

'Well, Jack, I remember a friend sharing an African saying: "If you think you're too small to make a difference, try sleeping in a closed room with a mosquito." Diseases passed on by mosquitoes probably kill about two million people every year. So, I don't think you can't not make a difference, Jack. It's just what kind of difference we make – that's the question.'

About half an hour later Jack told Grandad he didn't like the mosquito story. Grandad asked why and Jack said it made him feel sad.

'That's interesting, Jack. It wasn't the story that made you feel sad – it was you. Stories are information. It is up to us how we filter and react to them. I'm not too sure about that story either but if you feel strongly enough to be motivated to do something, then it's worth waking up and making it happen. Sometimes we're motivated by seeking to move away from things we filter as feeling bad. Sometimes we're motivated by seeking to move towards things we filter as feeling good. Often a mix of both of these results in our strongest efforts and achievements. If you notice how you and others filter and absorb information, Jack, you will learn much about people. You know, mosquito nets only cost a few pence.'

17. Mosquito nets

I've had an amazing week at school. On Sunday Grandad told me that mosquitoes kill millions of people in Africa and elsewhere. He said I made myself upset when I heard this. I suppose he was right but wouldn't everybody be upset? At first break on Monday I told my teacher and asked if our class could do something to buy mosquito nets for Africa. She said I could ask the class. I didn't usually speak out to the whole class but I thought I had to.

During break I thought about what I was going to say. I thought about what Grandad had said. I needed to make the children feel the same sad and angry feeling that I did. I thought I'd do it exactly like Grandad did. My talk went down really well and our class decided to do something positive. One boy even cried after I spoke because he thought of babies dying. Two other children suggested we should raise money for other charities but when it came to a vote even they voted with me.

By the end of the week the whole school was talking about mosquito nets. Everyone seemed as determined as me to make a difference. This has been my best week at school ever.

18. Not carrots and sticks

I told Grandad about my best week at school and he said he was really proud of me. He said when it rains some people stay outside, angry at the weather, and some people find shelter and think about their next move.

I told him about the boy who cried when I spoke about mosquitoes and he said I understood something about people most adults don't understand. He said adults think motivating someone is about offering them a carrot or a stick. They spend most of their time looking for the right kind of carrot or stick. They are looking in the wrong place. It is better to help people go inside of themselves and use their own carrots and sticks. It is much more effective and much quicker than presenting people with what you think should motivate them.

19. Billie Jean King

After Sunday tea the adults would sometimes play cards together. They only played for coppers but sometimes became quite animated as the competitive nature of some would kick in. Jack enjoyed the banter and gentle ribbing that flew across the room. Grandad rarely came off second best from verbal sparring matches so when he did Jack remembered the exchanges well.

The banter was much like a tennis match and appropriately on one afternoon around Wimbledon fortnight the conversation turned to the female tennis players. Grandad was teased that he fancied Billie Jean King. He defended himself by saying he admired her personality but this was returned with laughter and 1970s-style innuendo too crude to repeat until the post-ironic 1990s. He quoted the tennis star as an attempted verbal ace: 'I look on defeat not as failure but as research.' The effect was more like a double-fault as double-entendre was flighted back his way.

Later that day Jack asked Grandad about the exchange and his grandad asked Jack to remember what Billie Jean King had said because it was one of the six universal truths he'd discovered. Before Jack could ask about the other five he was asked to put the hens away for the evening and check for eggs.

20. *Negative or positive thoughts?*

Jack asked Grandad why people could be so hard to influence. Grandad said he liked keeping animals because they are generally easier to motivate. He supplied their food and used this to motivate his animals.

'With people you can look for a strong motivator. I've noticed if you want people to act quickly, moving away from a perceived danger works well. This makes sense. If there's a fire you need instant motivation to escape the danger.

'The first time I put this idea into practice was when I was nine. My brother and I once sneaked into the girls' changing rooms at school. The girls were in the showers but could hear us giggling. They knew there were boys hiding in the roof but not which boys. They said they wouldn't move until we left. We'd risked being told off for no benefit. My brother promised me two weeks of his pocket money if I could think of a way to get the girls to come out of the shower and into the changing rooms. I told the girls we'd been asked to kill the big spiders that were hiding in the girls' showers. The girls started screaming and running at the same time. My brother was so impressed he didn't mind giving me his pocket money. I've known since then that fear motivates people in the short term.

'If you want to motivate people over a longer period of time it's best to offer rewards and prizes that make them feel good about themselves. Better still, ask people to identify the things they'd like to achieve that would make them most pleased and satisfied. The people I've asked have given different answers but each person knows their right answer.'

21. *Curiosity*

Jack asked his grandad why there were so many fingerprints near the 'Wet Paint – Please Do Not Touch' sign but none further along the wall where the paint was just as wet but there were no warning signs.

'Because curiosity is man's greatest urge. It leads to all discoveries both helpful and unhelpful. Also, saying "please do not touch" tends to translate as "please do touch".'

Jack said he'd noticed this at school. When the teachers said "this test or exam was important but don't get nervous" he'd noticed that nearly everyone got nervous. Grandad agreed and also suggested that when someone says *but* in the middle of a sentence what they mean is the part that comes after the *but* is the only part that matters.

22. The Beatles at the allotment

Grandad occasionally played a little transistor radio while on the allotment. You couldn't hear it if you moved further than ten feet away. It was used mainly for test match cricket and football updates. Sometimes, when things were going badly on the field of play, he'd change to a music station.

The Beatles' song 'All You Need is Love' was playing. Jack asked if The Beatles had ever been to the allotment and Grandad took the bait.

'Absolutely, Jack. Paul sat just where you are now, John next to him, while Ringo and George played with the ferrets. Paul is one of the best weeders I've seen. They were taking a break from touring because they were tired of it. They wanted to develop musically and record studio albums. I told them to go for it but I couldn't help as I'm more of a lyrics man than a music man.

'We challenged each other to sum up all the wisdom in the world in as few words as possible. They'd travelled all over the globe and had met many wise people. We tried with one word ideas first and John suggested "imagine", "peace" and "love". Paul came in with "one world", "we need love" and "we are love". George went off to look at the hens and returned saying "Look, I am the eggman!" They'd laid four eggs. They eventually settled on "all you need is love". I suggested "all we have is love" because sometimes love isn't enough. Sometimes we can't control the destinies of others. Sometimes war, accidents and disease get in the way. Anyway, their version was quite a big hit.

'On the way out I suggested to John that he think about writing a song around the word "imagine", I don't know if he heard me. I later named some hens after the lads.'

Jack looked at the hen named Mandela but didn't ask.

23. *A light buffet*

Jack mostly saw his grandad at the allotment or at the house for Sunday tea. The christening of a relative's baby neither of them knew was the first time they'd met in a church. The place was cold and unfamiliar and Jack sat next to his grandad. The ceremony was thoughtfully reproduced in shocking violet on a bander-copied sheet of A4 using a religious font style, so they could follow events along with the other relatives that rarely attended church. Neither sang along but they mimed respectfully. Jack thought his grandad looked silly in a shirt that appeared to have been ironed in total darkness, a suit that was probably a good fit fifteen years ago and a tie that he was sure he'd seen at the allotment tying up some sweet peas last year.

Afterwards they all went back to the relative's house and had a buffet that was very much like a normal Sunday tea but, as this was the posh side of the family, there was quiche and salad – and it was called a light buffet rather than tea.

The next time Jack saw Grandad he asked him what he thought of the day. Grandad said he liked the improvised words spoken by the vicar. Jack sought clarification as he couldn't remember any of his words.

'He talked about light and dark, Jack. Light illuminates us and everything around us. It means we can see the beauty and horror of the world and the beauty and horror of the people within it, including ourselves. We can only see the best of the world and ourselves in the light. In the shadows we don't see beauty and we might think we're protected from seeing the worst things but we are not. If we are in the shadows we actually see more to be scared of as we imagine far worse dangers than are actually there. What do you remember?'

'I remember your tie and your suit, Grandad,' he giggled.

24. The white horse

A beautiful, white one-eyed horse lived near the allotments. Jack and Rosy enjoyed going to see the horse. Sometimes it would come over to the fence and they could stroke and pat its nose or mane while feeding it clumps of grass torn from the hedgerow or a carrot or some mint smuggled from home. On other occasions the horse would ignore the children and gallop across the field. Grandad said it was showing off. All animals have a natural grace and beauty but horses seem extra special. Their form and movement have inspired generations. The horse had lost an eye after an attack from a gang of boys. This, coupled with its sumptuous creamy white colour that changed to a greyer shade with flecks of black when close up, made the horse particularly beautiful. Even a swish of its tail was as graceful as the movement of a ballerina.

On their way to visit the horse Jack and Rosy were looking out for good, dark green tufts of grass to feed the horse.

Rosy asked Grandad how old should you be before you have a boyfriend. It was occupying her thoughts because she'd overheard Aunt Joy say to a neighbour that all men were a waste of time and women would be better off on their own. Grandad recognised the source of Rosy's question and observed that Aunt Joy might be better on her own but that is not necessarily true for all women. This did not help Rosy. Grandad then shared the wisdom his Mum had passed on to his sister. She said, judge men by how they treat you not by how they say they will treat you. Men will promise you all sorts. Notice more what they do rather than what they say. Grandad offered this advice to Rosy and suggested it could be equally useful to Jack. They had reached their destination and today the horse was feeding in another part of the field.

Jack had not heard Grandad talk much about his own Mum so he seized the opportunity to find out more. Jack asked if Grandad had ever been in real trouble with his mother.

'She only got really mad with me once. I was fifteen and one evening she asked me if I'd ever drunk alcohol. After I'd said no, twice, she smiled and congratulated me. She then asked me to fetch a bottle of beer and asked me to pour it out for her as she'd like to relax now

Horse with one eye

she had completed all of her jobs for the day. I carefully tilted the glass and poured it slowly and carefully so it would not froth up. After I'd poured it with the skill of a toothless old barmaid she took a long, slow sip. Then she put the glass down and told me off for lying to her and drinking under age.'

'How did she know?' asked Rosy.

'Well, because I'd poured beer a few times I was pretty good at it. I learned from her that what we do says more than what we say we do.'

By this time the horse had seen the group, remembered they were friendly and had trotted over to see what food they had brought.

25. *Choices and abilities*

Jack was remembering his Aunt Joy's funeral. It was the first funeral he had ever attended. After the service and food, Jack and Grandad walked up to the allotment. Jack noticed the funeral buffet was very similar to a birthday tea but with flowers instead of balloons. As it was his first funeral he was generalising that flowers replaced balloons at all funerals. He tried to imagine a funeral scene with balloons and novelty gazoos with their unrolling paper being blown around the coffin but it seemed incongruous.

'Are you sad?' Jack asked his grandad, keen to break the silence as they approached the allotment.

'I'm sad for Joy. She chose to have a miserable life. She chose it. Although she was a Star she didn't burn very brightly, but we all can. That's why I'm sad. Did you know that when she was young she was a very talented runner? She had more talent and potential than anyone else in the whole school. It's often those with the most to gain who resist and deny their potential. You notice this, Jack. It's an amazing pattern in people – as predictable as the pattern in a pigeon feather or a fern leaf. I'm sad for Joy because she became far less than she could have been. I watched her for years and for her, fear of success was greater than fear of failure.'

'What about you, Grandad?'

'Someone once advised me to be wrong often but only to be wrong in the same way once. It took me a while to understand what they meant but I've given myself plenty of opportunities to learn.'

Jack looked a little confused and nearly walked into an overhanging tree branch because he was concentrating so hard. He instinctively raised an arm to protect his face. He looked at his grandad and they both smiled.

'What I mean is you automatically raised your arm there and did so in the way I've taught you to block in karate – with the fleshy part of your arm facing the object moving towards you. If you block with the bony part of your forearm, either side of your wrist, it will hurt and you can easily fracture your arm. It's a learning experience the first time but breaking your arm ten or twenty times just would be annoying. By never going out for a walk Joy didn't break her arm. Think of all the amazing walks we've been on, Jack. Learning and living involves risk. The most successful people don't avoid risk; they learn from their experiences.'

They entered the allotment and Grandad asked Jack to remember three funny things about his Aunt Joy. Jack recalled some of the dreadful birthday presents he and Rosy had received from Aunt Joy. They'd laugh until tears rolled down their cheeks after they returned home. They had to try really hard not to laugh in front of Aunt Joy. Her knitted gifts were particularly bad: jumpers, scarves and even socks. You could itch in every part of your body while wearing her outfits.

Then Jack remembered a story he hadn't told Grandad. 'Oh, one time, well you know she went on and on about her illnesses? Her toes, feet, arches, ankles and basically every part of her body up to her flaky scalp and thinning hair. Well, when we were on the way home on the bus, and it was full, Rosy asked Dad what piles were. Everyone on the bus heard and looked at Dad and Rosy. Dad went so red and looked like he wished he could be invisible.'

Jack and Grandad laughed together.

26. Greasy Alan

Jack was cutting back a hedge. It was the first time he'd been given the job and he was warmed by the responsibility and trust. He'd pictured what the hedge would look like after he'd finished but the reality was not turning into the same picture.

The effect was similar to the time he'd cut his sister's fringe. In an attempt to create a perfectly straight line across her forehead he gradually cut away more and more fringe to balance out previous mistakes. A celebrity hairdresser he was not but his sister seemed fairly relaxed about the whole process until she looked in a mirror. Pity it was the day before her birthday party. Still, they laugh about it now.

His grandad came over and could see disappointment written across Jack's face.

'Don't worry, son,' he started.

'I was trying to get it perfectly straight.'

'Look, I've never seen a plant or person grow perfectly straight. They don't. They adapt and grow to suit their environment. Beware perfection, Jack. Do you remember Greasy Alan?'

Jack nodded as he handed back the heavy trimmers.

'Well, when Greasy Alan was a young man he was the most hand-some bloke in the village. He could have had his pick of any girl because he had everything a girl could wish for: height, brains, humour, good looks and an orange Ford Capri. But he decided to find the perfect partner. It became a quest. He searched all over the North-East, from Consett to Crimdon and Alnwick to Aycliffe. He rejected beautiful women with imperfect personalities and smart but plain girls. I met him once at a party with a stunning girl from Pelton who was as funny as she was beautiful. He later told me she had an annoying laugh. Anyway, he spent years looking before he finally found the perfect woman.'

'But isn't Greasy Alan old and single?' interrupted Jack.

'Yes, the thing is, he found the perfect woman but she was looking for the perfect man.'

After a break Grandad showed Jack how to use the trimmers. He soon got the hang of it and between them they'd done a good job. Jack asked Grandad what word he would use to describe the hedge now if perfect was not the goal.

Sensing his confusion Grandad replied: 'Don't confuse skill and perfection. Many people muddle up the two. Some excuse their lack of skill as modesty or saying "it'll do". It's often just laziness. Skill is a great thing to develop, Jack. Remember when we watched that starling build its nest last year? It was amazing, wasn't it? It was born with some knowledge of how to build a nest but it was skill that made it look so good. The bird had to choose from the material around and carefully place each twig, wisp of moss, and do you remember, even some of the fluff from the hood of your parka to create a beautiful nest?'

27. Present

Jack was excited. This was the first time he had bought his grandad a birthday gift. He'd wrapped it well and wanted to hand it over when they were alone. Grandad could see Jack's excitement and decided to build up the atmosphere by shaking the present, smelling it and assessing its weight as if it were a valuable old antique. He unwrapped the gift slowly. The paper fell away revealing a wooden frog that fitted neatly into the palm of his hand. It seemed to be hand painted and had ridges across its back. He examined it and it became clear to Jack that his grandad didn't know what to do with it.

'Should I show you?' helped Jack. Grandad passed the frog over and Jack took out a stick that slotted left to right inside the body and rubbed it across the ridges of the back revealing the perfect sound of a frog croak.

'Isn't it good?' enthused Jack. 'I know you like frogs and I saw it on our school trip.'

Grandad seemed a little distracted to Jack. Grandad was disappointed in himself because he hadn't figured out how to use the toy. It took the imagination and persistence of a child to solve the problem. The conservative adult approach had been fruitless. Grandad had been given a much better present than Jack realised.

28. *Walking with Paul Daniels*[3]

Walks in the winter were usually shorter. However, some of the best walks were on the dry, clear, sunny days following snow the day before. Although the route of the walk was familiar the covering of snow created new interest and challenges. Grandad promised games and puzzles on winter walks to tempt the children away from the warmth of the fire.

A long, old stone wall separated one part of the wood from a golf course. The children occasionally found golf balls that must have belonged to golfers who needed more practice. They threw the balls back over the wall aiming for a long shallow pond that ran parallel to the wall. If they threw a ball into the water and could hear a splash they won a prize. Today it looked like the pond was frozen over and snow covered much of the golf course. Grandad decided to share a challenge explained to him by Paul Daniels as there was little chance of finding golf balls or making a splash today.

The whole family enjoyed *The Paul Daniels Magic Show* and would try to figure out how the effects were created. Paul Daniels taught Grandad that the mystery and story of a trick was far more interesting than knowing how the effect was achieved.

'Your challenge is to hit the wall with a snowball. You take turns and have three each. The winner is the person who hits the wall from the furthest away. You decide how far from or close to the wall you stand. Is that clear?'

Jack and Rosy nodded and ran off looking for a source of snow that would create the perfect snowball, not too dry, not too wet. Jack asked to throw first and did so from a long distance from the wall. He launched his throw with a determined grunt but his snowball brushed against a branch and collapsed as it fell to the ground. Rosy chose to throw from the same place and her weaker throw missed the tree but still fell short of the target by ten metres or so. Jack had been visually surveying the area to make sure he hit the target this time. He moved past the tree and stood about ten metres from the wall. His grandad reminded him that if he threw above the wall that did not count. Jack threw confidently and judged his throw well but

---

[3] Like Derren Brown with a glamorous assistant.

his snowball sailed just over the wall. Grandad had been whispering to Rosy and she walked forward until she was only two metres from the wall and threw. She cheered as the snowball smashed into the wall leaving a white trace after it disintegrated on its way to the ground.

Jack thought over his last throw. He eventually settled on a spot clear of shrubs around four metres from the wall and hit the target easily. His excitement was tempered by the feeling he'd played it safe and could have done better. Rosy had an easy decision to make. She took aim one centimetre behind Jack's third throw. Before she threw Grandad called them over and said the game was the same as the game of life. They listened but would have preferred to complete the challenge.

'In life we have a choice to play it safe and not test ourselves. We'll hit targets but not ambitious ones. If we overstretch and take big risks we stand to win or lose more. Practice and skill help us choose a good distance. We'll only know if we're successful just after we've thrown. Now you go and have your third throw, Rosy.'

Butterfly seen near pond

29. *What do big girls talk about?*

When Rosy started secondary school she had been looking forward to finding out what bigger girls talked about. She only had an older brother and she couldn't think of any uses he had. She was aware of the concept of a pecking order because she had seen it in different animals at the allotment. She was disappointed in her conclusion that the older girls mostly talked about how fat or not each other was and how fat or not other girls were or were not. She didn't know if Grandma would know much about modern teenage girls but thought it could do no harm to ask. Rosy asked just before she was handed a spoon and bowl that had dollops of cake mixture left around the base and sides. Rosy thought the mixture tasted nicer than the cake it made because the flavours were concentrated and intense, and even better when she knew she had beaten Jack to the treat. Grandma offered an opinion.

'I don't know if the girls are too fat or not, Rosy. I do know that worrying about something is a waste of time. Do something about it, if you can, like deciding how much of the cake mixture to eat, or move on to thinking about something else. Otherwise you're just wasting life's opportunities. It would be like throwing away the cake mixture. My sister Anne worried about her weight. She was losing weight. Turns out she had cancer and did something about it. They caught the disease quickly enough and she was fine. So, would you like the mixture?'

Rosy decided to lick the wooden spoon first and let Jack have the bowl. She wondered why the mixture tasted better from the wooden spoon.

30. *Travelling*

Jack asked Grandad if he'd ever been to London. He said that as a boy he'd spent a month there staying with relatives. He loved the contrast to Durham.

'The children would go out exploring all day. We went to the docks and would see ships unloading their cargo. We could usually smell what the contents were before we saw it. One day tea, coal and fruit arrived and were carefully unloaded to be sent on. Huge deliveries from all over the world were arriving in London. It made me dream of travelling when I was older and was why, later, I joined the merchant navy. There was an atmosphere of excitement and activity that made you thirsty for more. It reminded you that Britain was an outward looking country. We were at our best as a nation when we were explorers and travellers.

'London was ours. We trekked all over it. We felt like we could walk on water and in St James's Park we almost did. The lake was sectioned off with concrete walls about six inches below water level for cleaning access. We ran across these pretending to be Jesus to the astonishment of onlookers. As long as you didn't get caught by a park keeper who would give us a clip round the ear.

'One day was a day of dares. They got more and more dangerous as the day wore on. The last dare was to see who could sit longest on the escalators on the Underground. One lad, Jimmy, mistimed his effort and got his bottom caught in the cold steel jaws at the summit. He had to go to hospital but when he came out he was famous and didn't mind showing off his scars to anyone brave enough to look.

'I've loved travelling throughout my life and despite the contrasts it was the similarities between people that were most noticeable. I've found that to be true wherever I've been, Jack. People are basically the same. They are kind, hospitable, proud of where they live and keen to build a place safe for their own families to flourish. The best way to understand the world is to meet people yourself and listen to them.

'Like most people of his generation my Dad never went abroad. The furthest he managed was Wales, to the Llangollen International

Music Festival. I think he went three times but not till quite late in his life. He loved going. It is an international festival, started in 1947 to heal the wounds of war. Musicians from across Europe came to compete. My Dad told me that when a German choir walked onto the stage there was a nervous silence because nobody knew how they were going to be received. Anyway, after a brief pause, the whole crowd cheered and applauded. The choir members had to go off stage for a little while with tears in their eyes because they were so moved by the warmth and hospitality of the crowd. My Dad met people from Europe and all over the world. He came back with great stories about the colours, costumes and strange musical styles he'd encountered. I think the festival still goes on today, Jack.

'When ordinary people meet you see the truth. We're all the same and we're all different. I hope you travel to discover this for yourself.'

31. Ghost story (1)

On longer walks Grandad would share ghost stories with Jack and Rosy. Most ended in laughter but occasionally an uncomfortable story would linger a little longer. Woods can be magical places. There are so many shadows and partly concealed branches in the shapes of claws and demons. There are unseen birds darting from shrub to shrub and sudden changes of temperature to quickly chill the blood. Dead animals, only spotted when a fizz of flies rise in a black swarm which quickly melt into the background of leaves and shrubs, create the perfect atmosphere for Grandad to create a ghostly story.

Grandad sat on a fallen tree trunk in a circular clearing and told of the time he was joined on this very trunk by the Grey Lady of the Wood.

'She had come to offer advice. She warned me that many people fear Death. They look over their shoulders and catch a glimpse of him. They are afraid to look him in the eyes because they will see their own eyes reflected back. They will see their own lives and be afraid – not because they see how they are going to die but because they see how they haven't really lived. She told me that the death of a child is greeted with more tears in heaven because of unfulfilled potential – each tear an adventure or achievement that will not be lived. The Grey Lady said we can all see Death when there is a moon visible during daylight. Even if it is just revealed briefly through the clouds, it is there to guide rather than frighten us. I asked if it's best not to look into the eyes of Death. The Grey Lady said only those that live their life fully need not fear Death. I asked if *she* saw Death and she smiled.

'The Grey Lady floated up into the trees and said it was worse than that. She had seen her future and ignored the prospect presented to her. She saw herself and her children and how she'd loved them far less than she'd loved herself. Instead of changing she continued a selfish life. Death has punished her by making her wander these cold woods looking for the children she had neglected. Sadly she didn't know what they looked like but she'd been searching for over a hundred years. "I see many children in these woods," she said, "and try to help by presenting them with clues to the future they will live."'

Grandad asked Jack and Rosy to look out for signs left by the Grey Lady on their way home. Rosy found a golf ball and thought this meant she was going to be very lucky in later life. Jack saw a bird's nest with three chicks. The parents were feeding the chicks. The parents would fly off collecting food and return every sixty seconds or so. Jack asked if it would be OK to move close enough to see the chicks. Grandad said it would be best to take a closer look when the parents were collecting food. When Jack moved in he saw one of the chicks was much smaller than the others and felt an affinity towards it. He didn't say anything to Grandad but thought this was his message from the Grey Lady.

32. *Richie Benaud*

While listening to cricket on the radio with Jack, Grandad heard a commentator talking about Richie Benaud. He pointed out to Jack that no one seemed to have a bad word to say about the man, even though he was an Australian.

Grandad told Jack what a fine cricketer he had been. As captain and batsman he had excelled but his leg-spin bowling was his specialism and passion. He remembered Richie Benaud being asked why he didn't write a book on how to be a great leg-spinner and his reply had been 'because everything you needed to know could be written on a side of A4 paper. You can pass on the theory in an hour but mastery through practice can last a lifetime.'

Grandad said he'd always remembered that as the best definition of wisdom he'd heard: 'When someone really understands something they can explain it simply and realise that understanding is just a new starting point. Beware experts who make things sound complicated and confusing. It is unlikely they are really experts.'

33. FA Cup final day

The FA Cup final was a really big event in the 1970s. Live games on TV in those days were a rarity and the build up to the final lasted a whole week. TV specials like *It's a Knockout* were filmed with supporters of the two finalists competing against each other. The whole Saturday was one of the best TV days of the year for Jack. By the time 'Abide with Me' was sung just before kick-off the excitement was almost unbearable. Jack and his friends would have Subbuteo[4] tournaments to help predict the score in the forthcoming final. Thankfully, real footballers never experienced the type of injuries sustained by Jack's table-top players. Two broken legs could be treated quickly with sticky tape to allow the player to continue. Two of his players had even lost their heads but they bravely played on. Modern players take note.

Dogs, not tackles from behind, caused the worst injuries in Subbuteo.

A popular PE teacher at school asked Jack and three of his friends for a favour. The school was competing in an athletics competition and needed students to make up the numbers in events for which the school had no entrants. The teacher explained that the school had some very talented athletes but to have a chance of winning they needed pupils to compete in all events as even a last place finish gave one point to the team. Jack and his friends were not exceptional athletes but they did play for the school football team and could

---

[4] Like GameBoy, PlayStation or XBox version of football games but it took far longer to set up and your dog could run into the room and ruin a game in seconds. My dog once ate Kevin Keegan.

probably collect a few points between them. The teacher reasoned that he did the lads a favour by giving up his time to run the school team in which they all played so they could give up one Saturday for him.

The plan was fine until the lads realised the day in question was FA Cup final day. They discussed it among themselves and agreed football trumps athletics. What could they say to the teacher? On each day of the week preceding the event Jack's friends all went to see the teacher individually and gave excuses as to why they would miss the athletics event – weddings, christenings, funerals. When Jack went to see the teacher he decided honesty was the best policy. He told the teacher the real reason why he wouldn't be jumping into a sandpit littered with dog poo that Saturday, and the teacher was furious. He said he'd be very upset if Jack let him down. Jack did let him down and the teacher did not speak to him again. He was dropped from the football team whereas his friends remained on good terms with the teacher.

When he told his grandad he asked if he'd done the right thing. His grandad said only Jack could know the answer and it would come from inside of him and not outside of him in the reactions of others. Later Jack told his grandad he thought he should have gone to the athletics competition.

34. *Leek sleepover*

Jack was really excited about his first sleepover. He was allowed to stay overnight at the allotment with Grandad who was guarding his leeks. There had been a spate of leek related attacks in the area and, as Grandad thought he was in with a shout of winning at the Leek Show this year, he thought it inevitable that he'd be targeted.

He and Jack were well prepared. They'd erected the old tent in front of the cree and had sleeping bags, a lamp and enough egg sandwiches to last about a week. They both completed chores until dusk. They settled in the pigeon cree porch and were reassured by the sounds of the pigeons behind them. Jack had never seen the allotment in relative darkness and was fascinated by the new shadows and noises all around. Seeing something familiar through new eyes is as rare as it is valuable. It was to be even more memorable as the clouds broke revealing a massive dark blue void peppered with stars blinking randomly across the sky in all directions.

'I love looking at the stars, Grandad. I sometimes look out of my bedroom window if I wake up in the night to look at the stars. The sky is so big and quiet.' They both looked up at the vast sky. The stars were confident, certain and reassuring. Stars make imaginations dance.

'I sometimes think, Grandad, that the stars are there just for me. I walk between those stars imagining what kinds of planets spin around the stars and what sorts of plants and animals might live there. Some plants with leaves as big as a house, some planets with yellow skies. I can travel to the edge of the universe in my imagination. You can't get there in a bus or a rocket.'

'Me too, Jack. I also think each star is a piece of knowledge, a piece of wisdom and I'm trying to figure out what they all mean. Perhaps one day someone will solve the puzzle and fully understand. Knit together all there is to know. Perhaps you can, Jack? I think it's when we keep our heads in the stars and our feet on the ground, then we can be our best.'

Jack often remembered this moment he shared with his grandad. The night was remembered by everyone else as the occasion when they were the worst security guards in history. Later that night, as they slept soundly in their tent, someone broke into the allotment and damaged the best leeks.

Grandad's magic
Leek mix

35. Ghost story (2)

Last weekend I had a sleepover at the allotment. I had a great time. It's really exciting being out in a tent all night. Grandad thought he frightened me with a ghost story but his snoring was scarier than his ghost story. I woke up a few times in the night but I think that's because it was cold. Even though I was warm inside my sleeping bag my face felt cold. I had to rub the end of my nose to warm it up a bit.

The moon was bright and when I breathed I could see my breath and imagine I was a dragon or a smoker. The pigeons made the most noise but it was quite a relaxing and reassuring purr. I heard a few noises which sounded like the birds shuffling about in their cages or animals foraging in the hedgerow.

It was late before we got inside the tent. We could see bats flitting around near the cree. They were silent and very fast. This was the first time I'd seen real bats. Grandad said they weren't silent because they made clicking noises which helped them to locate the position of their food. I knew dolphins used a similar system. I wondered if bats were as clever as dolphins. It was then that Grandad told me a ghost story.

Grandad's ghost story was of a wasp man who could inject you with fears that would grow inside of you and paralyse you in your life-defining moments. He must have remembered my biggest fear was to be paralysed by a wasp after seeing a programme on telly about it a few years ago.

36. Bruce Forsyth

Jack's favourite programme was *The Generation Game* and he often chatted to Grandad about the families and the challenges they'd faced the previous night. He had suggested that Grandad and Aunt Joy could be contestants and they agreed that even Bruce Forsyth would struggle to make Aunt Joy laugh.

Inevitably, Grandad told Jack that he'd met Bruce on a couple of occasions. While touring theatres before he found TV fame Bruce had stayed in a B&B nearby. Grandad met Bruce in a department store buying underwear. He had confided in Grandad that as a dancer he needed very tight pants. He also stuck to a rigid fitness regime. He didn't drink too much and didn't like the company of people who needed to drink alcohol to be happy. He was tired as he hadn't slept well in his digs. He'd complained to the landlady that the bed was uncomfortable. But her reply was that she'd only recently bought the mattress and had no complaints from the only other person to sleep on it – a magician who specialised in lying on a bed of nails. Grandad said Bruce was a true gentleman and professional. He worked hard to nurture the skill he had and to make the most of it. 'I said to him, with your attitude, Bruce, you'll have a long career.'

Bruce also passed on a thought to Grandad. He said he enjoyed hosting *The Generation Game* because it brought families together as well as the nation that watched the programme together. He thought the world was moving apart despite it becoming a smaller place.

'Take dancing as an example,' said Bruce. 'People dance apart now at these disco club places. In my time people danced together. They would hold each other and look at each other while they danced. They would have to get to know and trust their partner. There's too much dancing alone.'

37. *A focus of attention*

Jack was feeling down because a teacher had been giving him a hard time. The only thing he thought he had in common with this teacher was that they both found so much of school boring and pointless.

Jack was digging over a patch of soil ready for a potato crop. His grandad could see Jack was distracted. That was why he'd asked Jack to do some digging. But Jack's heart wasn't in the task. Grandad called Jack over and presented him with a challenge.

'I've hidden my penknife somewhere in the garden – the silver one with a red stripe. If you can find it you can have an ice cream. Deal?'

Jack immediately found a focus of attention. He looked around and planned out his optimum route for a search. He started at the top of the allotment by the pigeon cree and worked his way diagonally down towards the pond. He turned over pots and bricks revealing woodlice and fat worms but no penknife. He checked the plants bordering the pond, noticing that some were in flower and others had started to seed. He checked by the pond and was extra careful as he passed the leek trench, thinking Grandad would not have hidden the knife there for fear of Jack damaging a leek. He examined the fence between the allotments and noticed how much life relied on simple planks of wood. Earwigs slotted into gaps and spiders had created webs between the posts and planks where gusts of wind might blow insects into their trap. He noticed the trenches he had been digging were rubbish. They were supposed to be in neat rows of alternating mound and hollow so the potatoes could be dropped in at just the right depth. Instead it was a random mess.

After around half an hour or so Jack gave up and returned to his grandad: 'I can't find it.'

'You haven't looked in the best place to find things. Look in your pocket.'

Jack felt inside his pocket and could feel the metal and the shape of the penknife: 'You tricked me!'

'When you were digging the trench your attention was inside your head when it should have been outside.' They both looked at the trench which confirmed the statement.

'When you were looking for the penknife your attention was on the outside when it would been more useful to go inside. Choose the right place to focus your attention for the task in hand and you'll be alright. Now go and dig the trench properly or we'll never get an ice cream today.'

38. Real education

Jack announced at teatime that he didn't like school. Jack didn't normally make such statements. Later, as they walked to the allotment, Jack admitted he was being bullied.

Grandad said there had been a lot of bullying at his school but in those days it came mainly from the teachers. Jack too had got on the wrong side of a teacher. Jack had been sent out of the class for 'smiling disruptively'. 'He says I'm not a good student. He says I'm useless. Am I useless?'

Grandad responded by saying he wanted to show Jack something. He went over to the pigeon cree, scrabbled around in the big, old chest under the bench he'd made and came back carrying something shiny.

'Look at this, Jack.' He handed over what looked like a military medal. It was quite heavy too.

'I was given this war medal by your great-uncle Frank. He said I could keep it if I could find out its true value. I didn't think much about the medal until we studied the First World War at school. I took it in and first showed my friends in the playground. One lad offered me a pound for it. Good money that. Then I showed it to each teacher who would let me and one valued it at £10. The last lesson was history and Mr Phillips was really excited when I showed him the medal. He told me and the whole class all about it. It was worth over £100. Now I know that not all good teachers realise the true value of medals but all good teachers should know how to value children.

'He also told us this: during the war pilots were not given parachutes. They knew if they crashed they would go down with their plane. The pilots accepted this. The reason they were not issued with parachutes was that planes were very expensive and the RAF wanted the pilots to do everything they could to return rather than bail out. Later in the war they realised that pilots were harder to train and replace than planes, so parachutes were issued. I know how valuable you are, Jack, and the only real purpose of your education is for you to discover your true value. It'll be loads more than you think and if one teacher can't see it look out for those that can.'

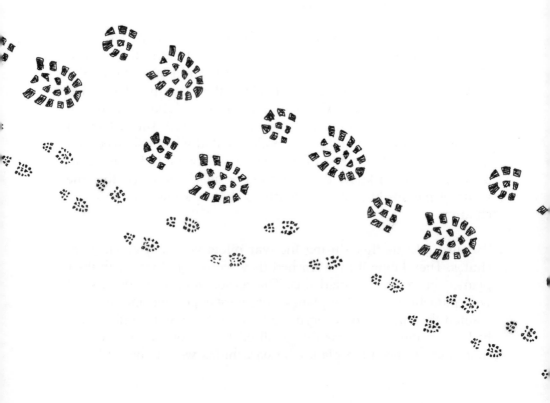

39. *Mountain climbing*

Jack asked his grandad what was the best job he'd ever had. Grandad told Jack how he'd been chosen out of twelve climbers to become the next leader of the group. The test to find the new leader had involved a long and difficult climb. The old leader led the way. He told each of the climbers they were nearly at the top and the next peak would be the last so to keep going for a little bit longer. As they all pulled themselves up over the ledge where the leader sat he looked at their faces. One after the other they arrived exhausted on the ledge. Each one looked at the instructor and then up to see even more cloud-covered mountain ahead, and each sighed in frustration. The leader clearly saw the disappointment on their faces.

Grandad knew he wasn't the best technical climber or even the strongest climber so he asked why he was honoured to be chosen as the next leader. The instructor said it was because when he reached what he thought was the top of the mountain, only to see another peak covered in snow and cloud, he was the only climber to smile at the instructor and say, 'Wow, there's even more.'

'I think I've been a little like that in everything I do, Jack. I think you're the same. You think, "Wow, there's even more." It's a great attitude to have. Make sure you climb plenty of mountains.'

40. Doing the right thing

Tom, the owner of an allotment further down the hill, came over to see Jack's grandad. Tom thanked him because Jack and Rosy had helped his granddaughter earlier that day when she had lost her doll. They'd helped her find it and then taken her home.

Grandad was going to share the story of the lion and rat when the children arrived. A hungry lion trapped a rat beneath his huge paw but then decided to free the rat and wait for a bigger meal that would satisfy his hunger better. The next the day the lion was caught in a net left by trappers. He swung helplessly from a huge tree. The rat he'd freed earlier climbed the tree and chewed through the rope. After a few minutes the rope gave way and released the lion.

Perhaps he didn't need to share the story.

41. Alan Bennett's last meal

Jack hadn't heard of all of the famous people his grandad talked about. He'd never heard of Alan Bennett but thought he sounded like an interesting man. Grandad often talked about the power of words and how many people were careless with the words they spoke or didn't pay full attention to the words that were offered to them. Jack asked his grandad: 'If you could have anything for your last meal what would it be?'

Grandad said he'd asked Alan Bennett the same question when he'd come to the allotment to pick up some broad beans. Alan's reply was, 'Oh, I don't know, probably a slice of date and walnut cake with a cup of tea.' When I suggested that this wasn't a particularly indulgent or reckless choice for a last meal, Alan replied, 'Well, if I knew it was going to be my last meal I don't think I'd have much of an appetite.'

Grandad continued the story while shaking out the blanket that covered the old sofa in the cree. 'I gave him a recipe using broad beans that he later said was "good enough to be on any menu, even one's last".

'Listen carefully to the words people use, Jack. Ask yourself are you listening or just waiting for your turn to speak?'

42. *Bounty*

Some Sunday afternoons were spent in the house if the weather was too cold or wet. TV films often became the focus of attention. Jack liked watching films with his grandad because they'd talk about them later (and sometimes during, which really annoyed Aunt Joy while she was still alive). Jack remembered *Mutiny on the Bounty* having a big impact on his thoughts. The captain ruled by fear and fear alone. He interpreted the rules to suit his aims. Jack was amazed that one bad man could have so much power over a large crew.

Bounty

Later, the family took in a rescue dog. It was a greyhound and they can be nervous animals at the best of times. This greyhound was not a good enough runner and had therefore been poorly treated. When she arrived she quietly quivered and shivered in fear, cowering under the table away from the adults. The dog didn't have a name until Jack suggested Bounty. He remembered the film and was determined to help the animal grow in confidence by showing it the opposite of fear. Jack did really well with Bounty as he had the three things required for nurturing her: time, patience and love.

Bounty went on to become a blood donor dog which meant Jack's dedication helped many more dogs than just Bounty.

43. *Beer mats*

Grandad broke a silence as they sat on the ledge of the leek trench by announcing he had something for Jack. He pulled out a couple of beer mats from his coat pocket which he handed over. 'Have you got either of those?'

'No,' replied Jack as he examined the beer mats and straightened out a crease in the corner of the larger one.

Jack had been collecting beer mats for about six months. He built his collection by asking the adults he knew to bring him any new designs they encountered and also went into pubs himself and asked for beer mats. He was usually greeted with enthusiasm and then quickly sent on his way with a couple of pristine beer mats from behind the bar.

Children were not allowed inside pubs and were usually left playing outside if their fathers had offered to 'take the kids from under their mother's feet for half an hour'. Mum would no doubt be aware of the hoax due to the smell of pub on her husband when he returned but such games are the bedrock of many relationships. Working men's clubs were the poorest source of mats. The doors were usually guarded by a skinny old bloke in a cloth cap who took his role very seriously, which was mainly to prevent women and children entering the bar area. All he had guarding the entrance was a wobbly old table and a wall of cigarette smoke – Jack had only once obtained a mat from one of these men.

Around half a dozen other lads adopted his hobby because he'd taken some of the more interesting ones into school. He would swap copies with the other lads and their collections grew quickly. The Hoffmeister 'Follow the Bear' mat was the most sought after because the advert on TV was popular. As neither local football team was in the First Division this seemed more interesting than collecting football cards. Some weeks Grandad would ask Jack if he'd learned anything interesting or useful since they'd last met.

As Jack carefully placed the mats in his pocket he commented: 'I've noticed, Grandad, that some of the lads have far more beer mats than me even though I've been collecting longer.'

Grandad suggested they may have more alcoholic family members but Jack said he thought he'd figured out the real reason. 'I only swap mats I've got copies of whereas the two lads with the biggest collections will swap all mats. Sometimes they'll get three new ones for one rare one. I thought it was better to only swap mats I had copies of but I think I'm wrong.'

'Well, Jack, it sounds like you've learned something useful.'

44. Penalty shoot-out

Jack and Grandad would sometimes play a penalty shoot-out using the hens' pen as a goal. It was a perfect size at around one metre high and three metres wide. Jack usually won as he was prepared to dive no matter what the condition of the ground. If it was bone hard or muddy puddles it didn't matter – he just got covered in a different kind of dirt.

The only time Jack struggled was in the midst of the big match atmosphere. If they were pretending to be deciding a World Cup final, Jack would sometimes 'bottle it'. Grandad noticed this and passed on some advice that Jack decided to use in a number of ways in the future.

'Jack, I'm going to pretend to be your manager now offering you advice, OK? Imagine I'm the best manager in the league, Brian Clough, having a quiet word before the UEFA Cup Final. You can be yourself. It's normal to get nervous when we feel under pressure. What we must do is move above that pressure. Imagine the pressure is like a slate grey cloud. The bigger it is the further you have to rise above it. This is fine because the further you rise the stronger you become. Once you've risen above it you are as strong as you can be – think of strongman Geoff Capes and imagine what it would be like to be as strong and focused as him. Now you're ready to make yourself proud. Not just yourself proud, though, your children and grandchildren will hear about this day from you and how great you were.' Jack looked bigger to his grandad. He smiled and said he was ready to play.

England won the World Cup.

Grandad had previously told Jack to think about something that always made him laugh for times when he wanted to relax. He chose to think about Aunt Joy in nettle knickers. Now he had two ways to deal with nerves. Two ways to do something is much better than one way. It means we have choice which means we have control.

45. *Walking with David Attenborough*

During a walk Grandad was pointing out things Jack and Rosy hadn't even noticed – rabbit droppings, a deer footprint, nests tucked away in trees. He thought it was important that we pay attention to and understand our environment. Jack said he was like David Attenborough.

'That's because David Attenborough came on this walk with me yesterday and pointed out many things new to me.'

The rest of the walk involved a closer examination of the plants and animals they encountered. Grandad even whispered some of his observations in classic Attenborough style and gave furtive glances left and right in case gorillas or wolves were close.

Grandad said what he liked most about David Attenborough was his knowledge of humans. 'I think he understands people as well as he does animals. After the walk he came back to the allotment to look at the pigeons. He was talking about the big choices we make in life. Sometimes we know a decision is a big one. He was Controller of BBC2 and had been very successful in the role. He had a choice to be promoted within the BBC or to go off and make wildlife documentaries. Both options had merits. One had status and was safe, respectable and logical. The other was more of a risk as no one had really made a career out of animal documentaries. What should he do? He sought advice from his brother. His brother asked him to choose the option that made him feel more excited. This is good advice. He closed his eyes and imagined the first option and noted how he felt. He imagined himself sitting behind a desk, being important, making decisions about what programmes other people would make. This felt OK. Then he closed his eyes and imagined the other option. He pictured himself in jungles and deserts and mountains, places most people can never visit. The vivid colours overwhelmed him and he felt excited. His choice was made.'

46. *Walking through time*

Grandad had an interesting challenge waiting for Jack at the allotment. He'd set out a line along the path between the allotment gate and the pigeon cree representing Jack's life. Right now they were standing at the leek trench not too far from the gate, the point which represented the present. The allotment gate behind him was the moment of Jack's birth. His future lay ahead of him towards the pigeons.

'Will you play this game, Jack?'

'Yes, what do I do?'

'First, think about someone you admire. Someone who has had an impact on you recently.'

'That's easy, I saw the film *Little Big Man* last week and I loved it.'

'Great, why did you like it?'

'I loved the main character. He really enjoyed his life. He went through life as a learner. He had loads of interesting experiences. He joined an Indian tribe. He met famous people throughout American history. He was also small, like me, but it didn't stop him being brave and strong and wise.'

'Close your eyes and think ahead to yourself as an old man. Think of yourself as ninety-nine years old. Picture you've had a brilliant life, the best life you could possibly have. Imagine you have all the qualities you admire in *Little Big Man* within you as you walk through your successful life. Let's walk along until you age that much, all the way to ninety-nine. Imagine how you feel as you mature, getting stronger and bigger as you become a man, then notice the changes you feel as you age. Notice the achievements you make along the way and how they make you feel. Note which things make you most proud of yourself. In fact, notice everything, Jack. Think about what you'd really like to achieve.'

As Jack walked the timeline he had a strange experience. It was great and powerful. He felt that he grew stronger and wiser. On the way he married and had children. He saw his children look up at him and smile their love to him. They loved Jack as much as he loved Grandad. He couldn't see what career he'd had but he felt he was good at his job and people lined up to thank him for the help he'd given. It made him buzz and glow. Grandad asked him to look at his achievements from when he was ninety-nine back to himself as a fourteen-year-old. He asked Jack what linked all of his life together and he felt it before he could say it. It was a warm, strong, tingly feeling that went through each step he'd walked linking them all together. Wow, it felt good.

'What advice would you send back to Jack to make sure he has his best life?'

'Go for it. Enjoy the journey.' As Jack said this he shivered with excitement as if a sparkler was fizzing through his body. Afterwards Grandad asked him to write down that evening what he'd experienced and to use it as a guide. He said Jack should keep it, and he did.

Watering can and hat I bought
at a Jumble Sale for 20p

47. Barking (3)

Jack enjoyed bringing Bounty to see Grandad. It was a chance for him to see how good Jack was at looking after an animal. Jack would excitedly provide updates on Bounty's developing strength and confidence. Today Grandad suggested they take Bounty for a walk to the wood. Jack immediately thought of the barking dog and asked if there was an alternative entrance to the wood.

'No,' said Grandad, 'I want to go past that house. It's a surprise. Come on.'

They set off on the walk and although Jack trusted his grandad he grew more nervous as they approached the house. He didn't want Bounty to sense his nerves so he thought of Aunt Joy in nettle knickers. Jack noticed a difference as they approached the house. The high fence had been replaced with a smaller slatted fence and you could see into the garden. A large lawn lay in front of an old, red brick house and clothes were flapping from a washing line. He'd imagined a gothic castle full of witches and goblins behind the fence. A dog scampered over towards the three walkers. It offered a friendly yelp to Bounty who responded by pressing her nose between two slats. They stayed for a while and then continued the walk.

'Jack, you're great with Bounty. You have a talent with animals. It's great to discover the things you're really good at. Well done.'

Jack thought this was the best walk he'd had.

48. Successive approximations

Grandad rarely left Jack and Rosy on their own at the allotment but on this occasion he had to go and help a goat give birth. He'd asked the children to plant out a couple of rows of lettuce seeds while he was away. They stuck to their task despite a heavy downpour that washed away most of their efforts. When he returned, instead of being pleased they had stuck to the job, Grandad seemed annoyed.

'Plans are plans. And you are both human and have amazing brains. With a plan and a brain you can be flexible; you can adapt the plan to suit the circumstances. It's amazing how many people just stick with a plan, often someone else's plan. You'll meet many people like this. Please don't be that kind of person. But also don't be the opposite, the kind of person that has no plan. What you want is flexibility.

'I want both of you to grow up having plans and flexibility. Not like the man who decided he'd like to bungee jump even though he didn't have the proper rope. He used normal rope. He tied one end to his foot and the other to the bridge. He jumped and to begin with it was great. By the time the rope was fully extended he was travelling very fast and stopped suddenly mid-air. His foot was ripped off as he fell the last ten feet slowly. That was because the ripping of his flesh and the tearing of muscle, skin and tendons took a couple of seconds. He was lucky to survive. You wouldn't do that would you?'

Jack and Rosy were unlikely to ever plant seeds during a downpour or bungee jump for a long time.

49. *Grandma's rugs*

Rosy asked Grandma why she made 'proggy mats' (rugs made from rags). Rosy had seen five in the kitchen, one in the bathroom and a couple at the allotment. Grandma explained that she used to make them with her own Mum and still makes one each year. She showed Rosy how they were made. A wooden frame holding thick hessian formed the base. A large hand-held needle with a hook at one end and a wooden handle on the other (a progger) was used to pull strips of unwanted material through the hessian. Only after Rosy had tried using the progger herself did she appreciate Grandma's skill.

Grandma explained that prior to central heating the mats were essential. They began life on the beds to keep off the worst of the winter cold. After they lost their freshness they were relegated to the floors. Grandma asked Rosy what she thought of the rugs. Rosy noticed a mistake in each one and asked why.

Grandma was impressed with Rosy's keen eyesight. Grandma noted that her husband had only once commented on a rug she'd made. It was black and white and he'd refused to have it on the bed until she had added red flecks. Grandma told Rosy that she deliberately made a mistake in each mat because if she made a perfect mat there would be no point making any more.

50. Jack's favourite childhood toy

When people ask what my favourite toy is I've usually answered before they finish their sentence. Grandad made me a go-kart. He was always collecting bits of wood and metal. He was friends with the man who owned the bicycle shop. Once he got four tyres, two each from the front of damaged Tomahawk and Chopper bikes, and we made the best go-kart ever. The tyres gave a smooth ride even on the cobbles. The axles were metal poles. The back wheels were fixed but the front ones pivoted from a central point with a loose rope attached near each wheel. When pulled back from the sitting position, an old cushion secured by more rope, steering was possible. But at high speeds I just hung on trying to keep my eyes open.

Our street ran down quite a steep hill and there were rarely any cars. I placed obstacles to add skill and drama. I played with a lad I didn't normally play with, Ally, the pig farmer's son, because he had a watch with a second hand. So with his watch we could time each other down the course to find out who was holding the world record. When I held the watch I could smell pig on it but I didn't say anything to Ally.

We both became very good and agreed even Barry Sheene would not have been able to beat us. We played every weekend for about a month or so. Grandad had to make many repairs to the frame and Grandma many repairs to us. We grazed and bruised our arms and legs. Ally once got his foot caught between the front wheel and frame. I thought he'd broken it but a gulp of water from the kitchen tap seemed to sort him out. I still have a scar on my forearm sustained from a particularly brave world record attempt. Broken glass and dog poo littered the hedge side running down the right-hand side of the street but you had to aim for this side if you were going to crash because on the other side were people's houses and some had big stone steps. We both boasted we didn't fear a bad crash because we thought we might be whisked off to hospital to be rebuilt like the Six Million Dollar Man.

I remember the go-karting really vividly. This is still one of the top five experiences of my life. I wonder how many brilliant experiences people average in their life? I must make time to add more.

51. *Perception is reality*

Grandad often gave Jack and Rosy questions to think about while they completed a task. The question today was: which African animal bigger than a mosquito killed most people each year? The job was to move two wheelbarrows full of compost to the leek trench where he would add a secret ingredient before spreading it across the soil. They discussed the question and completed their task efficiently.

'What's the answer then?' asked Grandad. He was holding a clear plastic pop bottle half full of a straw-coloured liquid with a green tinge. Jack offered crocodile and Rosy lion as their answers but both were wrong. Even a second guess each did not deliver the correct answer. Grandad had to convince the pair that the hippo was the most dangerous large animal. They're usually portrayed as cute or clumsy in children's stories which belies their aggressive nature.

Jack asked what the secret ingredient was in the leek growing mixture in the bottle.

'That's what I wanted to share with you today. Perception is reality. You would be more scared of a crocodile or a lion than a hippo, yes?' The children nodded as Grandad poured the liquid across the compost he'd spread in the trench.

'Our truth is what we believe it to be. The other leek growers think I have a secret formula that makes my leeks the best. The result of that belief is that I don't think they believe they can grow a better leek than me. I've won for the past three years since I accidently told one of the men I had a secret formula. What do you think is in the formula?'

'Hippo wee?' suggested Rosy.

Grandad winked as he whispered, 'No. Keep it a secret, but it's just water I've left in this bottle for a month.'

'But the secret ingredient in the pigeon food is real, isn't it?' queried Rosy.

52. *Your hardest day's work*

'What's the hardest day's work you've ever done?' asked Jack.

Grandad thought for a while. 'When I was a lad we'd help the local farmers get the potato crop in. They paid about twenty pence for an eight-hour shift. You were bending down most of the time and before long your whole body was exhausted. I've never felt as tired since. Every muscle wanted to stop you. The jokes with your mates kept you going. I slept really well those nights.'

'Why did you do it, if it was so hard?' queried Jack.

'Well, we were told to by our parents. The farmers needed to harvest the crop or we'd all suffer if the potatoes rotted in the ground. What I remember most though is the feeling, *if I can do this I can do anything*. We have to stretch ourselves, Jack. What's the hardest day's work you've ever had?'

'I don't know if I've had any,' answered Jack honestly.

Later, Jack said he thought school was sometimes hard. Grandad asked him why. He supposed it depended mostly on which teacher was at the front of the class. If we are lucky we meet a teacher who inspires us to believe in learning as a way to find the best in ourselves and the best in others. Jack's was Mr Quinn, an English teacher from Ireland. Students left his classroom feeling great. He would read text using different accents – Welsh, Geordie and Cockney were his best. He'd also recite adverts from TV, sing jingles and, best of all, repeat sketches from *Not the Nine O'Clock News,* the top TV show for many teenagers at the time. Jack had to pretend to interview Gerald the Gorilla while Mr Quinn imitated Gerald almost as well as Rowan Atkinson.

Jack had told a few teachers that he'd seen the film *One Flew Over the Cuckoo's Nest* on video. Every teacher, other than Mr Quinn, said it was an 18 certificate film and he was too young to see it. Some even ranted about the evils of new fangled video players that exposed children to things they could not understand. Jack was pleased he hadn't admitted he'd seen *The Return of the Living Dead* zombie films. After he'd discovered most of the class had seen the film, not only did Mr Quinn ask Jack what he thought of it, he discussed the plot and themes of the film over the course of two lessons: How was school like the state asylum? How was working life like the state asylum?

Even the children who didn't normally join in class discussions were interested in the film's themes. Controlling people through externally imposed rules and procedures or manipulating them through shame, guilt and humiliation was widespread in Jack's comprehensive school. As was the practice of labelling people and the threat of violence lurking beneath the surface. Many students were also fascinated by the way drugs were viewed in the asylum as the cause of and solution to the inmates' problems. The patients were insulated from risk by accepting a removal of their choices. Jack had been moved by the film and by the end of these two lessons so had the whole class. Jack had not enjoyed school as much as this since he had persuaded his classmates to buy mosquito nets.

53. *The Hoppings*

Each year the Star family visited a big fair held in Newcastle. They caught the bus together with other excited groups. By the bus stop there was a dead hedgehog but that hadn't dampened the mood of excitement in the queue. On their way to the Hoppings Jack confided in Grandad.

'I don't know what to do after school. Some people know exactly what they want to do. Tony wants to be a footballer. Lisa wants to be a hairdresser. Ally wants to be a pig farmer. I don't know.'

'That's OK, Little Big Man, there's plenty of time to find out what you're good at before deciding. If you do it the other way round you're unlikely to choose the right thing for you. You have to remember to enjoy finding out. Don't treat it like a chore. Don't think your friends are better placed because they have one idea about their future. One idea leaves no choice and only choice offers us an opportunity for control in our lives. A hedgehog only has one real skill – rolling up in a ball. This has worked brilliantly well to protect it from foxes but isn't so useful against lorries and buses. If it had another option, perhaps sonar to sense vehicles at a greater distance, or wings, it would be more successful. Discover something you like, develop a skill and enjoy where it takes you. Remember to be open to new experiences and you'll adapt if you need to. Hedgehogs without twenty-first century adaptations don't do so well on roads. So people that can learn and keep learning are going to be successful.'

They arrived at the fair. It had rained for a couple of days so the town moor was as muddy as a cow field. There was more tension and excitement in watching teenage girls in high heels trying not to fall over in the lane of thick, deep mud than there was in the coconut shies and amazing sideshows promising sights to curdle the blood and terrify the weak of mind. Jack learned the secret of how Geordie lasses could go out on bitterly cold winter evenings wearing less material than can be found in an average tea towel. They exuberantly applied layers of make-up and false tan so thickly that it protected their flesh from arctic temperatures.

Before Jack realised, Grandad had guided him into a fortune teller's booth so he could have his future foretold. He now wished he hadn't said that he didn't know what to do when he left school. His only other knowledge of fortune telling was from his Aunty Barbara who'd had her palm read on a day trip to Blackpool. She was told she'd marry three times and have seven children. She was on her way as Uncle Brian was her second husband and she had five children. She'd also been warned to stay away from Welsh people by the palmist. She'd taken the advice literally as a few years later she declined the opportunity to see Tom Jones in concert when he toured the North-East. She missed a great night out by all accounts.

Inside the little booth were exotic looking drapes and letters of thanks from the stars of the day. Jack noticed signed photographs from Mike and Bernie Winters and Keith Chegwin[5]. No doubt their future health, wealth and prosperity were assured. She pointed to an old chair and Jack took his place while Grandad gave her five pounds and left. Like the time he'd had an injection at school he just wanted the experience to be over with quickly. She grabbed his arm and gazed at his palm.

'Ah, you have a strong lifeline, my boy.' She had a European accent not unlike his French teacher. 'You wish to know what your future will be? Your hand is not as strong as your imagination. You will become a wise man. You will remove confusion and fear from others. I know because you bring confusion and fear in here with you today and a person teaches best what he most needs to learn. You will be a great teacher.' She finished with a theatrical flourish by looking directly into Jack's eyes, 'You may ask me one question.'

Jack, feeling like a hedgehog before the wheel of a speeding truck, wished he could have thought of a better question: 'Should I avoid Welsh people?'

---

[5] Examples of 'stars' who shine then fade; like the people who appear on *I'm a Celebrity Get Me Out of Here* twenty years after they were famous and the Cheeky Girls.

54. *Hatching time*

As Jack and Grandad cleared up ready to go back to the house for a well deserved Sunday tea, Jack noticed a pigeon chick beginning to hatch. He'd seen this a few times but it was magical on each occasion. They both watched as the egg wobbled slightly from side to side. A small beak started to tap through the shell. Soon the chick was standing up tentatively, like the drunken old blokes Jack had seen walking out of the club on a Sunday lunchtime squinting at the light as they emerged from the doorway, and staggering as they suddenly realised how drunk they were in the fresh outdoor air.

Pigeon chicks are incredibly unattractive. Bulbous heads and wispy down feathers that barely cover their pink and veined bodies. Jack and Grandad thought they looked scrotal but both kept the thought to themselves.

'It's amazing how quickly they mature isn't it, Jack? Soon they'll be able to fly back to this spot from as far away as France. Mind you, Jack, you're growing up too. How old are you?'

'I'm sixteen.'

'You've learned so much, Jack, I'm really proud of you.' Grandad then told Jack five things he thought Jack had learned over the past month.

55. *Building a pigeon cree*

Grandad had hinted for weeks that he and Jack would have to do some major repairs to the cree. The most renovation Jack had seen over the years was the reapplication of paint along the front in red and white stripes. The pattern had to remain the same so the pigeons would remember where to return. Jack thought if they could find their way from France they would probably remember where the cree was. However, Grandad had so many trophies that he decided to keep that thought to himself.

The only time he ever felt in his grandad's way was on those days when pigeons were due back. He was allowed to stay but only if he was quiet. Anything that made the birds circle one more time before they landed and could be clocked could lose Grandad a winning place. His grandad would stand by the cree noisily shaking a tray with a little grain in it to encourage the birds to land without delay. Jack felt privileged that he'd been asked to help with the painting and repairs. Grandad had been collecting bits of wood for a number of weeks in preparation for the project.

There were no instruction booklets on how to build a cree. Grandad taught Jack as they went along.

'The framework is made from railings from the pit fences opposite the wood. And these parts were all made from orange boxes,' Grandad pointed to the relevant sections. 'You can't find orange boxes for love nor money these days. The roofing felt is fine but some of the frame is rotten, from the pigeon muck not removed properly over the years.'

Inside there was a roosting area with perching ledges and nesting boxes in another section. Jack asked about the flaps at the front and top of the cree.

'Those are clever things, Jack. They're a flap that can take the weight of a pigeon but snaps shut if something heavier, like a cat, attempts to enter.'

David's Grandad

Even grandads were young ...

Grandad asked Jack to sit on a big, old trunk while he found somewhere dry to put the wicker baskets used to transport the pigeons. Jack hadn't noticed the trunk before today.

Grandad asked Jack to saw a couple of lengths of wood while he removed the rotten pieces. He'd drawn in pencil exactly where he wanted Jack to saw. They spent about four hours working on the cree, including the repairs and the painting, and Jack had never been more proud of a day's work in the allotment.

'Right, Jack, what do you think of the quality of our work today?'

Jack thought for a while. His honest appraisal would be that, although they'd worked hard and produced a cree that would safely house the pigeons for a few more years, their craftsmanship was not really up to the standard of some of the other crees in the allotments. He decided to speak the truth as he saw it while mentally crossing his fingers that he wouldn't cause offence.

'I'm so glad you said that, Jack. Let's be honest, neither of us were meant to be joiners or painters. When you asked me what job you should do a few weeks ago I said the important thing is to find out what you're good at and enjoy it. Part of that is being able to identify what you're not good at without getting upset.'

Grandad said the sportsmen and women he most admired were athletes. He revealed that he used to work at the local track as a volunteer caretaker and couldn't believe the dedication of many athletes. They trained in all weather throughout the year. Footballers are sometimes called athletes as a compliment to their physical condition. Grandad thought it was right that athletes were placed at the top of the pile of sportsmen and women. He suggested we can all learn from athletes. They discover their best event from many choices and then they practice and develop their skill over many years, aiming to be their best.

Jack needed to try out a few ideas before trying to narrow down his choice of job.

56. *The Merlin factor*

Jack and Grandad were taking Bounty for a long walk. They'd taken her to open fields so she could have a good run about. Bounty loved the countryside where she could burst into amazing sprints.

'Isn't Bounty beautiful, Jack? Her body has been designed to run quickly and she does so with effortless skill and grace. Most dogs are bred to be great at one thing. I think humans have the capacity to be great at many things. You told me about your teacher, Mr Quinn. The best teacher I had was Mr Rowell. He told us stories about voodoo, shape-shifters, prophets and shamans – people and creatures through history that appeared to have magical powers. He told us of the rituals of clans. North American Eagle Clan or Bear Clan dancing into the night, dressed in bird and animal costumes, dancing themselves into a deep trance to discover what it is like to be these animals and gain a deeper understanding of their thinking and their environment. Mr Rowell would make us believe we were a raindrop, a comet flying through space or the string of a guitar to deepen our understanding. We had some amazing lessons.'

They sat on a dry raised clump of grass as Bounty sniffed around an unaccompanied terrier at the far end of the field.

'My favourite story was the legend of Merlin,' continued Grandad.

Jack interrupted excitedly. 'Yes, I remember in the Disney film *The Sword in the Stone* Merlin turns himself into a fish, a squirrel and a bird to learn more about himself and those around him. I do this when I play footy in the park. I pretend I'm different players. You know, a defender when I need to make a tackle, a winger when I want to run down the wing and a forward when I'm approaching goal.'

'Well, I'd like you try out the same idea in every area of your life, Jack. You have to imagine you are different animals and people to see what you can learn. I've learned so much from the stars who have visited the allotment or been on walks with us.

'The part of the Merlin story I like best, Jack, is the part when Merlin asks Arthur, as he is staring at the sword in the stone, 'What's the best thing that could happen now?' and Arthur says it would be pulling out the sword from the stone. Merlin asks him why. After a pause Arthur replies 'because if I could do that I would know absolutely that I can do anything I want to do. Anything.'

They made a deal. Jack would look at ways he could apply these learnings as three people he admired and so would Grandad.

57. *Sunday tea*

On some days Jack would spend time with his Grandma. She spent most of her time at the back of the house where there was a big built-in oven and fireplace. She seemed to be constantly preparing food or clearing it away. It was always hot in this room which made it a popular place in winter months. He was allowed to help out cutting and mixing pastry and mashing and mixing fillings for sweet and savoury pies.

His favourite job was licking out the bowls after the cake mixture had been spooned into the baking tins. Jack once asked Grandma if she ever got bored making the same food over and over again. She replied by saying she was pleased there was food to prepare as this hadn't always been the case. She also had her part-time job which gave her a change. She was a dinner lady at the local primary school. She also said she liked looking after her family. She didn't understand the younger generation who were obsessed with 'finding themselves' and indulging in sensory pursuits. Jack wasn't sure what sensory pursuits were but thought he could look it up in his dictionary later. She'd been brought up to provide and care for her family and she excelled in the role.

Grandma said her father and brothers had worked really hard in the pits but they just got on with it. She thought many people lived their lives these days resentfully. She didn't think that made any sense. She advised him only to have a family if he really wanted one and was prepared to help it grow and flourish. She told Jack she hoped his generation would make a better go of things than his parents' generation. He hoped so too as he finally understood something she was talking about. He definitely agreed that his grandparents seemed happier and more sorted than his parents or the parents of his friends.

He was quite relieved to get back to preparing Sunday tea. He was pleased to be given the job of buttering the bread. Years earlier he'd been advised to move the butter nearer to the fire to soften it, then it spread easily. Grandma gave him a wink, pleased he had remembered her advice: 'Well done, Jack. Do things right.'

58. Tony Marbles

The king of marbles in the area was Tony. The fact that he was known to everyone as Tony Marbles gives you an idea of how good he was. Basically, he was so good that no one would play him for keeps. I thought I'd try Grandad's Merlin game and challenge Tony Marbles for keeps! Quite a crowd gathered round. I imagined I was Tony and copied his stance and flicking technique as I watched him warm up with a match against Ally.

I used his own techniques when I played Tony in the next game. And to my surprise the strategy was working. I could see Tony becoming annoyed. The crowd leaned in. I was two marbles up then I started to notice the boys around me and lost my concentration. I was bottling it. Three minutes later, deflated and defeated, I went up to the allotment to see Grandad ten marbles lighter.

Later, I told Grandad what had happened and he asked what I'd learned from the experience. I said not to be distracted and to stay focused. Grandad also said I should remember the Merlin game was something to help me learn more about myself and how I can be my best – not to compare myself to or try to be better than others. He said I should be aiming to be the best Jack Star I could be. He's said that a few times now.

59. *Victoria Beckham*

Rosy asked Grandad if Victoria Beckham had been to the allotment as she was interested in the concept of girl power and what it really really was.

'Oh yes, Victoria has been here. Just before the Spice Girls made it big. She begged me to join the group. She'd thought it all through. I was going to be Silver Spice. I said no and said they'd be better off going with an all-girl vibe. She tried to change my mind but I had too much to do in the allotment to be out conquering the charts. I think I was right, with my leg I'd never have managed the dance routines. Anyway I named a pigeon after her instead. See that skinny one over there looking in the mirror? Not that one but the one next to it.

'I remember she was a very clever person. One of the things she said was that success spreads like butter across hot toast. She's right, Rosy. All moods spread quickly in a room and cover it completely. So make sure you go for the moods you want to spread. Then you'll have real girl power.'

60. *My very last trip to Billy the barber's*

I remember the last time I went to the barber's with Grandad. I fancied a girl at school and wanted to get a really cool haircut. Grandad's barber only did one cut though – short back and sides. His only concession to customer care was that you could have it shaved at a number one or number two length, which looked the same. If I'd been going for an army interview I'd have looked great but I was going to school the next day. While I sat in the queue Grandad chatted to Billy, a good name for a barber, I thought. Mum had said I didn't have to get my hair cut here any more but I'd always had my hair cut with Grandad and I didn't want to let him down.

I thought about asking Billy for a different style. I was trying to think of a way to bring it up in conversation but as I'd never had a conversation with Billy in eight years it seemed a brave step to try now. All he ever said was, 'Bye, you're growing aren't you?' I thought about saying, 'No, as it happens, I'm getting smaller like the Incredible Shrinking Man' but obviously didn't. Could I ask Billy if he watched Top of the Pops? *He didn't look like the kind of bloke that would. Could I suggest he give me a Noel Edmonds-style bouffant or a Kevin Keegan perm? No, I couldn't.*

When I got home, Rosy, as always, said it looked awful – and it was deserved as she hadn't forgotten the time I'd cut her fringe.

61. *The rules of whistling*

Although I wasn't impressed with his barbering skills I was even less impressed with Billy's whistling. Like most men of his age he would burst into spontaneous bouts of whistling that could stop as suddenly as they started.

There were some unwritten rules around whistling: women didn't whistle, men didn't join in with another man to form a duet ending in interlocking arms and a wistful look into each other's eyes as they delivered the climax of 'Danny Boy' or the 'Girl from Ipanema', urinals were the best place to start and finish a whistle due to the superior acoustics, and the playlist was strict: nothing from Radio 1 or post-1975.

I was now sixteen and trying to understand the adult world I was inevitably moving towards. There were so many things I didn't understand. I'd more or less worked out whistling, I think, though I was far too young to begin whistling in public. I imagined that if I'd burst into a snatch of 'Karma Chameleon' at a urinal I'd have been run out of town before I could button up my flies.

Grandad had been brilliant but there were so many things we didn't talk about. I was neither a boy nor a man. What kind of life would I have? What should I aim for? Would I wake up one morning as an adult and know everything?'

62. *Elvis and Marilyn*

Jack was helping Grandad relocate the hen run. After six months or so the hens stripped the area of all vegetation. Moving it to an adjoining patch that had recovered and encouraged worms and slugs, as well as a little grass and a few weeds, made for happier and healthier hens.

Jack said he'd heard that Elvis had never set foot in the UK. 'Well, Jack, that's the official line but I mustn't have told you about the time he came over with Marilyn Monroe for a break.'

Jack said he couldn't recall the story and thought he'd have probably remembered it. 'They had a great time. They were both quite shy you know. They had to *turn on* their star quality. Elvis would do it on the walk from his trailer to the stage. By the time he arrived he'd be the big star. Marilyn did it through the *way* she walked. If she was out with friends they'd be surprised that she wasn't recognised by the public. Only when she did *the walk* did people then recognise her. Stars who don't switch off and have a way to be normal are those that struggle the most to live a contented life and find themselves. Many people go through life without ever finding the time or place to *turn on* their star quality. When you find yours, Jack, make sure you also find the off switch. Otherwise you'll just burn out like the patch of land in the hen run.'

'How do you turn it on and then off?' asked Jack, as he released the hens into their new run. They enjoyed exploring the new patch – scratching at the plants and chasing towards the few worms that were visible.

'I know how I turn my switch off and on. You'll need to find your own switch, Jack.'

63. *An interesting lift*

Jack hoped he would become as wise as his grandad. He stayed on at school and attended a placement in an engineering company, Trojen, during his first year. The firm manufactured lifts. For a week Jack had felt like an outsider because the staff talked in jargon and technical words he didn't understand. He even thought many of the staff didn't understand each other but didn't seek clarification for fear of appearing stupid. Jack didn't think that was a good a way to run a company but tried to remember he was there to learn not to teach. He especially enjoyed visiting a trade exhibition and comparing the different styles and features of lifts. At the end of the week he was invited to observe a board meeting.

'You'll learn something here, son,' said George, the patronising manager who'd spoken *at* Jack for most of the week. Jack knew a lot about the man but he knew very little about Jack. He knew George lived for just two things: work and tennis.

'We're going to discuss whether or not to invest in new machinery that will improve the performance of our range,' he continued, as they entered the impressive looking boardroom. Jack had never seen such a big table.

The meeting proceeded over three hours but it seemed much longer. Jack picked up the dilemma facing the company. Should Trojen risk investing in new equipment to modernise the products they manufactured or play it safe and stick with the current equipment which would work efficiently for another five years? The clincher was the combination of testosterone with research which suggested their competitors' lifts were faster than theirs. The decision was made: they would invest for faster lifts. Jack was not asked to comment until he'd left the meeting with George.

Jack told George he didn't think the company's lifts were slower than the competitors': 'The competitors have mirrors in their lifts which means by the time you've checked your hair, tie and flies you're at your destination. The journey only appears faster.' Jack thought it would be cheaper to put mirrors in the lifts rather than make them move faster.

George didn't say anything but Jack later found out the company had reversed its decision. He thought the company could benefit from mirrors not only in their lifts.

Jack sent a thank you card to George with a picture of a female tennis player scratching her bum. Inside he wrote a quote from Billie Jean King. (See story 19.)

64. Lisa

I was becoming both more and less confident. A programme on TV said this was normal for teenagers. The first proper girlfriend I had was Lisa. At times she was more confident than me and at other times less confident. It was a confusing and exciting time. I wanted her to meet Grandad. I wanted each to be impressed with the other so they would both be impressed with me.

What a disaster. Lisa thought the allotment was awful. She thought Grandad was awful. When I looked at Grandad through Lisa's eyes she was right. He was a sad old bloke growing stuff that no one liked anyway. She couldn't believe he grew potatoes when you can buy frozen chips. She even had a go at him. When she saw the pigeons she was unimpressed. She thought they were smelly, dirty animals and she told Grandad he should get rid of them because they spread disease.

I was surprised and disappointed that Grandad didn't stand up for himself. I don't know if he expected me to defend him. Lisa said she could understand my interest in Grandad when I was a little child but I was a sad loser not to grow up and move on. Lisa's world was exciting and different. Perhaps she was right and I should move on. Had I learned what I could from Grandad and was it time to be an adult like Lisa?

The more I tried to be like Lisa the less she seemed to like me. I thought just my sister was weird but perhaps it was all females. I'd never worn clothes that matched until I met Lisa. She thought there should be programmes on TV about clothes and make-up. I thought, surely nobody would watch that! All the certainties of my childhood were disappearing. I thought it would be best to stay away from Grandad for a while. I stopped going to the allotment.

65. Jumble sale

Jack had been forced to go to see his grandad as it was his birthday. He asked Jack if he fancied a walk to the village hall as there was a jumble sale. Jack was thinking he'd rather not but thought he could go along for a quick look as they sometimes sold cakes and teatime was a couple of hours away. They had a look around but there was nothing of interest. Perhaps they were a little too late. Timing is everything at a jumble sale. On the way home his grandad said he was thinking of a Chinese proverb he'd heard recently: 'When the winds of change blow, some build walls, others build windmills.'

66. *Bazza the coach*

Bazza the footy coach did some interesting research. He recorded what happened when a penalty was taken: what side the kick was struck, whether the keeper dived or stood still, dived early or late, whether the penalty was struck with power or placed, whether it was saved or a goal. He was hoping to advise his own keeper on the best tactics. He was amazed at what he discovered. He didn't believe it at first so he went back and checked all his files.

He discovered that the most effective thing a keeper could do was to do nothing. If the keeper just stood still he would save more penalties because many were put down the middle. Also by not diving it put off the taker as it's easy to place it after the keeper dives to the other side of the goal. Most keepers will not stay still though because they feel they should do something.

Jack thought the principle might apply in many areas of life. People prefer doing something rather than doing nothing. Even if they don't have a good idea they'd rather do something. Politicians, parents and teachers all seemed to be at it. They want to improve things so they do something. Jack thought he'd do something after he'd thought it through and had a hunch it would have a good impact. He thought he'd try to remember that sometimes doing nothing can be the best something you can do.

67. Cigarettes and alcohol

I went to a party with Lisa. The venue was a flat being rented by an older brother of one of Lisa's friends. It was very untidy and a bit smelly. A bit like my bedroom but on a bigger scale. I thought they were her friends but she said she didn't know most of the people there. I didn't like the atmosphere. It seemed to get worse when we arrived. Lisa's old boyfriend was there and one of the girls told me I was only there to make him jealous because Lisa wanted to go out with him again.

Lisa had gone into the kitchen with some girls. Her ex-boyfriend appeared to be different to me. He was surrounded by people and seemed very popular. I sat nearby to listen in to the conversation. Most of the people were smoking roll-ups. They offered me a drag and although I didn't want to I took it. I inhaled too much and as I coughed they laughed at me. I was feeling more uncomfortable and sick. To get out of the way I said I was going to the toilet. I passed more people drinking from cans of lager.

I didn't think this party could get any worse but when I came back through the kitchen Lisa's ex-boyfriend was waiting there for me. He was being egged on by his friends to get me. I only had a younger sister so I'd never developed good fighting skills. I knew he was going to hit me and time sort of slowed down. As I noticed my legs feel wobbly he punched me in the cheek. My whole cheek felt hot but it hurt in one place on the bone like an injection at the dentist.

The rest was in slow motion. He punched me again on the other side of my face and this time it hurt more because I was more scared. He pulled me down by the hair with such force I thought he'd tear it out. Some hair did come away wrapped between his clenched fingers. I was lying on the kitchen floor and I could feel and smell the dirty carpet tiles on my face. I tasted blood in my mouth and swallowed it.

'Kick him' shouted some of the mob. I don't remember being kicked. I remember looking up when the noise had gone and finding myself alone in the kitchen. I went over to the sink and looked in a small mirror wedged behind the taps. I looked OK. I scrubbed a little water around my face and slurped a bit and went home. My fighting career was over. One fight, one defeat. Not quite Muhammad Ali.

68. Cheek to cheek

The club's football team had a mid-season injury crisis. They asked a few of the under-18 team players to fill in and cover for some of the games that had been cancelled due to frozen pitches. In return for playing you were allowed into the club free after the match for a pint and the Sunday lunchtime enter-tainment. I only played the one match and we drew 2–2. The pace was faster than I had been used to and the swearing and aggression on the pitch quite scary. I went down on the team sheet as John McKnight and had been made to memorise his date of birth in case I was asked by the referee. The referee seemed more concerned about surviving the game as he took some serious abuse. He looked even younger than me. His legs were so white and skinny they looked more like dining chair legs than those of an athlete.

After the match the team showered and changed into their going out clothes. When I asked why they were patting aftershave on their faces they just laughed at me. I was offered the bottle and when I applied it, boy did it sting. I'd seen the Old Spice adverts on TV but instead of feeling like an Adonis surfing confidently through giant waves to rousing classical music, I felt like an awkward teenager with slightly sore cheeks.

The club was packed out for the Sunday lunchtime slot. It was like going into a dark cinema during daylight. The football team were allowed to sit at the front. They gave me the best seat. I realised why when the music started and a stripper came onto the stage barely five feet away from me and barely dressed. Tina Sparkle's act was a bit of a blur to me to be honest. She looked old enough to be my Aunty Vera and drunk enough to be my Uncle Tommy. I thought the lad I fought in the kitchen was hard but this woman was tougher than Geoff Capes. When she pulled off Billy the barber's wig he didn't dare complain because she gave him a stare that could win a war. I don't think I'll ever be able to look at a Union Jack flag in the same way after the way Tina used it in the finale of her act. I still wince when I see footage of children waving flags at the Queen. She wouldn't appreciate the sea of flags if she'd seen and touched what I had that Sunday.

So I had a glimpse of the adult world. I was so relieved John McKnight was fit enough to return to the team the following Sunday. In a month I'd lost a fight, a girlfriend and my Grandad, and found the feeling of fist, aftershave and Tina Sparkle on my cheeks.

69. Bonty night

Bonfire nights were big events in the village. Jack wanted this bonty to be the best ever. He was seventeen and knew he was drifting away from his grandad. His girlfriend Lisa had dumped him because she'd heard about the after-football entertainment. The real reason may have been because he was a wuss at fighting and she fancied having her old boyfriend back. Jack thought he'd try to remember events in a way that made him feel good. He wanted to attend the bonty because he thought this could be the last one. Each year fewer people attended as the safety messages on TV discouraged home-made bonfires. The village was changing and it was noticeable at key times of the year. On his way to the bonfire he'd noticed cars parked all the way along the street he'd once raced down in his go-kart. There wouldn't be space to race now.

He remembered the best bonty he'd ever attended when he was thirteen. Children collected wood for weeks and dumped it at the end of the field where the bonfire would be erected. Some of the men would slowly build it in the lead-up to the big day. It was exciting to see the bonfire rise slowly each day like a giant wigwam. Jack hid an old tyre he'd found in the middle of the bonty and looked forward to seeing the smoke from it. The challenge was to have a bonty that was still burning in the morning. This would win school bragging rights.

Around half an hour before dusk the men appeared and made the final touches to the bonty. At the last minute, unwanted wooden material was brought out. There was good natured laughing when an elderly widow, Mrs Jenkins, asked if two of the men could bring down the bed she'd had for thirty years. Her husband had passed away a month previously. The widow was in high spirits. 'Careful with it, lads, he was bedridden and incontinent for the last six months. It's a pity he couldn't have lasted until tonight – we could have thrown him on the bonty too. He'd have liked that, the tight old sod, saving on a cremation.' A couple of wardrobes and a hat-stand were also brought out. Grandad said it was like the *Antiques Roadshow.* A couple of guys were thrown on the top to a cheer from the crowd.

Traditionally, the fire was lit by the oldest person there at 7 p.m. Soon the heat made everyone stand a little further back. Once the fire settled some people tossed potatoes in. Jack hoped they didn't land too close to the tyre or to Mrs Jenkins's bed. Grandad produced some sparklers and he and Rosy wrote their name against the dark night sky. Jack wondered if he was too old for sparklers but he was enjoying himself enough to join in. The noise and spectacle of the fireworks rising into the sky in all directions contributed to the excitable atmosphere.

As the flames settled down and the crackling and spitting from the fire calmed to a reassuring maturity, everyone soon began to smell of smoke. Even those trying to second guess changes of wind direction to stay out of the smoke were undone by occasional gusts that seemed to want to dance in their own way.

Tonight's bonty was far more modest. This one would be out before midnight. Less than a dozen spectators. Many people had decided to attend a large organised display and some stayed in to watch TV instead. Jack remembered his Grandad once saying that when we change our minds we do so quickly. We think we're logical and clever and make decisions only after carefully weighing up evidence for or against but this is not how it really works. Jack had a flash of insight as he stared into the flames. He had thought he was changing and Grandad wasn't. He realised that wasn't the important thing. As a wave of warmth blew from the fire he realised he wanted to stay close to his grandad and would make sure they both continued to be learners and teachers together. Jack went over to his grandad and said he'd built his last bonty and was now going to build some windmills.

70. *Answering Lisa*

Jack asked Grandad why he hadn't answered some of Lisa's complaints and negative comments. Typically, he told a story instead.

'If she'd brought me a gift of a tray of still warm scones, fresh cream and strawberry jam falling out over the edges and I refused them, who would the scones belong to?'

'Lisa,' I answered.

'Exactly,' he replied.

He asked if the insults also belonged to him as Jack didn't defend him.

'Only you know the answer to that question, Jack. Take a look at history and examine the fate of those who stand up for the wronged and those who say nothing. A clear pattern emerges.'

Jack realised he wouldn't wake up one morning a fully fledged man. Life is a process. We grow and change a little bit at a time.

71. Rainbows

Jack worked in an old people's home while at university. The job took up most of his weekends. He was fairly comfortable around the elderly. He'd been brought up around ferrets, goats, hens and pigeons so he didn't mind the messy parts of the job. Some of the residents reminded him of his grandad. The residents were generally well cared for. His only negative thought was that many were unable to go out much. He did take some of the residents into town during his lunch hour in their wheelchairs. They were generally buzzing afterwards, able to share their adventure with those left behind.

Frankie was one of Jack's favourite residents. Jack told Frankie that he was giving up the job to see more of his grandad because over the last few years he hadn't seen too much of him. Frankie said he'd be missed but thought it was a good decision. Frankie asked if they could go into the garden. They sat on their favourite bench in the garden on a beautiful day that supplied all four seasons in an hour. A rainbow flickered above a row of houses on the other side of the park that ran parallel to the home. Frankie and Jack exchanged views on what gold would be found in the pot at the end and whether there was a pot at each end of the rainbow or just one end. Frankie stopped joking and suggested that Jack remember the pot of gold is not at the end of the rainbow, it *is* the rainbow. They both looked at it again, strong and fragile, vibrant and opaque, fleeting and eternal. For a moment they were the rainbow.

72. A night at the club

Grandad was working on the door at the club while Tommy, the bloke who normally did the job, was 'under the hospital'. Jack presumed this was a euphemism for male orientated surgery, but didn't ask. Years ago Tommy gave Jack beer mats for his collection. Jack said he'd pop along to keep his grandad company. He sat in the corridor with Grandad and they each nursed a pint.

Jack got to know some of the characters and ended up quite liking the atmosphere.

Working men's clubs took a lot of stick for being out of step with the wave of feminism that was moving across Britain, but the wave was weaker in the North-East. Women were not allowed in the bar. This especially annoyed the sort of women who wouldn't want to be in these bars. Jack realised that the men, who used to work together in the pits, had transferred all the bravado, tribalism, genuine respect and affection they shared when they worked together to these smoky male-only rooms. There was rarely any aggro. Club legend had it that there was only ever serious trouble once, following a Keith Harris and Orville gig. Apparently, when the police found out who had headlined the evening they felt it was sufficient provocation for the mini-riot in which Old Derrick lost his glass eye.

One old bloke, Jonesy, was criticising 'southerners'. The general drift of his polemic was that they were selfish. The fact that he hadn't travelled south of Darlington during his whole life slightly diminished the credibility of his argument but there were many quick to concur with Jonesy, though not Grandad.

Grandad talked about his time doing national service. He shared his stretch with men from all over the country and said they all got on well together. The mining communities did bring people together in the North-East and some parts of the country lacked the focus of a pit area but he said that you can't generalise that all southerners were one thing or another.

As the discussion had started after each man was on his fourth or fifth pint, the debate lacked some clarity and incisiveness but this was more than compensated for by the energy and loudness of the contributions. In an attempt to calm things down a little, Grandad asked if he could recount the time of the biggest dispute among the men. The noise ebbed away as he settled into the story of the marble-topped commode.

'In 1960 Princess Margaret was engaged to marry Lord Snowdon. Squaddies were given the option of contributing one day's pay towards a wedding gift or donating blood. This caused much resentment and discussion in our group. Most of us went off to give blood for the first time in our lives. We were soon stationed in Belgium and in return for an armful of blood given to the Red Cross you received coffee, biscuits and enough money for two good nights at the pub.

'I still give blood today and the blood is not sorted based on which part of the country you were born. We all had a choice to make: to give blood to those who would need it or to give money for a small marble-topped commode for the royal couple. The choice we made then was based on our values and upbringing which pointed us in the right direction – and this is more important than where you're born.'

Later that evening the quiz resulted in a tie for first position. The quiz master, Old Derrick, took a lot of stick throughout the evening for his lack of flexibility over answers. 'Hey Derrick, I think your glass eye is rolling under the table' was a common distraction method as various fellow team members attempted to distract him to sneak a look at the answers. The top prize was only a pint each but this did not blunt the competitive edge and faux rivalries that had built up over the years.

73. *A holiday in Cyprus*

Jack's favourite holiday was the two weeks he'd had in Cyprus after finishing university. It was the first vacation he'd shared with his girlfriend Anna. In the first week they travelled inland and visited Nicosia and the mountains. In the second week they stayed along the southern coast near to the sea. It was lovely to be able to cool off in the afternoon in the sea as the heat was so unfamiliar to him. Perhaps he was hallucinating as he lay on the beach drying off in the shade. He craved cloud. Even a little grey wispy beard of cloud would be reassuring. He almost felt greedy and guilty that he was able to enjoy such uninterrupted sunshine. He'd noted that climate definitely affects culture. The Cypriots were as warm and generous as their climate. Apart from when they got into a car. They'd not heard the expression, it's better to be late to arrive in this world than early to arrive in the next.

One day they decided to take a boat trip with a group of other tourists. For a reasonable fee, Yiannos, the boat owner, would take them along the coastline to his family's restaurant. They would be fed and returned via a secluded sandy beach where they could relax and enjoy the sea and scenery. There were nine people in their group: two couples in their mid-twenties, one British and the other Australian, plus two Cypriot women in their forties, Jack, Anna and a self-made businessman from Stoke-on-Trent.

The forty-minute trip along the coast was fantastic. They were close enough to the shore to see the landmarks they passed, described enthusiastically by Yiannos. The breeze created as the boat cut through the water cooled and refreshed the group in the heat as they enjoyed the sunlight fracturing and fizzing into thousands of jewels that wrapped around the boat. Later the group shared an authentic Cypriot meal of many courses blending all the culinary traditions of the region. A local wine with a hint of aniseed flavour softened the mood of the group as they fully relaxed into the day. Afterwards they made their way to the beach and it was as stunning as Yiannos had described at the start of the day.

On the beach, Brian, the self-made man from Stoke-on-Trent, revealed he'd lost his first wife to pneumonia and his second wife to a bingo-caller from Burslem. He spent much longer talking about a mould-injection-something his company had developed which had made him financially well-endowed. He took it upon himself to offer business advice to Yiannos, first suggesting he raise his prices. Yiannos replied that they were adequate to cover his costs. He then suggested Yiannos buy a bigger boat and hire someone to take the trips for him.

'Why would I do that?'

'You'd then earn more money.'

'What benefit would that give me?'

'Mmm, you could retire early and do whatever you wanted.' Brian was struggling a little now but he was not the sort of chap to give up. 'How would you spend your time if you'd retired?'

'I would buy a little boat, take visitors to eat with me at my family restaurant and eat with them, then visit my favourite beaches along the coast on the way back. Then I'd ride back home on my motorbike and see my family again.'

Brian was quiet for the rest of the trip, possibly figuring out an appropriate way to spend the rest of his retirement.

74. Grandad's CV

After we returned from Cyprus, Anna and I couldn't wait to tell Grandad all about our adventures. As we studied locally we saw Grandad regularly. He'd taken a shine to Anna and seemed to enjoy the opportunity to share stories about the celebrities he'd advised. I'd heard many of the stories before but didn't mind hearing them again. There were also new stories. Grandad had invented rap during a visit to New York and had been instrumental in the decisions of Michael Palin and Billy Connolly to change career direction and consider making travel documentary programmes. Once Anna got to know him she realised these stories were a sign that dementia wasn't setting in, rather than it was. The allotment was still the focus for Grandad. The pigeon racing had stopped but he still kept the pigeons and the hens. Grandad's world seemed to be changing but not as fast as the rest of the world. Even though I'm twenty I'm still happiest at the allotment, sitting on the porch of the cree, listening to Grandad, his voice like a warm blanket.

I asked him why he liked comedians so much, as many of his stories featured comedians. Sure enough he quoted Michael Palin from one of their recent conversations. It is their honesty. Comedians seek authenticity, they aim to describe the world as it really is and people as they really are, with all the raw absurdity, hypocrisy, magic and awe laid out before us. They are the opposite of many politicians who describe the world how they want us to see it, through their self-fulfilling blinkers. Some politicians are intent on taking us somewhere they say is better, forgetting we are already in the best place, here. He then showed me a quote he'd written down and asked me to find the source: Seeker of truth, follow no path, all paths lead where truth is, here.'

75. *Get knotted buns*

The holiday in Cyprus had a bigger impact on myself and Anna's lives than we had first realised. We'd spoken about marriage, living together and children but not this soon. After we got used to the idea of being parents in our early twenties instead of late twenties, we started to see the benefits as well as the disadvantages.

Anna organised most of the wedding herself. The only job she gave to me was on the morning of the wedding day. I was to drive into town and collect an order of sixty knotted buns for the reception which would be held at her Mum and Dad's house. I drove down and entered the shop and confidently asked for the order of sixty buns. The lady serving said she didn't know anything about the order. I explained that my wife had already ordered and paid and I needed to be on my way. She checked with a woman in the back of the shop. This woman, Betty, also knew nothing about the order. After a short pause they gave me the buns and hoped I had a great wedding day. When I relayed the events to my new wife a few days later she worked out that I'd been to the wrong bakery.

76. Wedding day advice

The wedding was a brilliant day. Grandad was on top form. He said, 'I've only been married once, unless you count Britney Spears. What a weekend that was.' He also said, 'I'm proud of you, Jack. Anna is a lovely girl, not as nice as that Lisa girl though.' I was surprised he remembered Lisa but then realised he knew more about me than anyone else, including Anna.

I told Grandad he'd be meeting his great-grandchild in around six months time and he looked as happy as I'd ever seen him. He hugged me and then pulled back saying he didn't want us to be crying today. I said I'd already cried after I'd seen him turn up in the same suit and tie he'd worn at every family gathering through the years. I joked that I'd take him back to the allotment so he could secure his sweet peas with his tie again.

I received advice from Anna's Mum and Dad. Anna's Mum was a bit of a hippy. She'd travelled around India in the sixties and looked like she'd left some of herself there. Her Dad was a more typical Northern man. He'd built a successful commercial window cleaning business and was doing very well. Our families supported the same North-Eastern football team which meant the wedding date didn't clash with a home match.

Anna's Mum sat next to me at the reception and offered me some wisdom she'd learned about while travelling in India. 'Jack, there are six forces. Energy. It can flow from inside of us out into the world or it can flow from the world into us. Both are important, use both at the right times. It can be hot or cold. It is called many things such as anger, peace, nerves, fear, confidence and charisma.

'Reality. There is rock, mountain, sea. This is the real world. We need to respect it and nurture it. It is the earth. There is also our imagination. It is like the rainbow, brilliant and magic but cannot be touched. It is when human imagination touches the real world that there is magic and alchemy.

'There is one and there are many. We are either alone or together. This is community. Islands appear alone until you look under the sea and realise they are all joined together. There are no separate nations.

'There is chaos and there is order. We seek to understand by looking for an underlying structure which provides comfort and a path to follow. It is illusionary. It is just a direction to take not the truth. It is a view not the only

view. The view out to sea is satisfying and provides much understanding but turn around and there is an alternative view with different answers and questions. There is constructive and destructive. We can build up or knock down. We can seek to be a force for good or a force to serve only ourselves.

'These five forces are the infinite from the nothing. Time and space create the above as delightful illusions – the sixth force in which the others move as puzzles for us to ponder. Time and space for each of us is a blink. We only get to dip our toe in this stream at one place and time. Our own understanding is washed away as quickly as it occurs to us like the water flowing down the stream after we remove our toe.'

We then shared a knotted bun. Much of the day was spent moving from one place to the next. Before the disco started Anna's Dad took me to one side and said he would like to pass on only one piece of advice.

'Relationships are all we have. You can either make your relationships stronger or weaker and thus yourself stronger or weaker. Simply ask yourself three questions before you pass on any information about one person to another. First, are you sure it is true? Second, is it positive?

'Finally, is it useful to the person with whom you're going to share it? If the answers are negative then so too will be the impact on you, the person you talk to and the person you talk about. You will all be weaker. If the answers are positive then the impact will be positive for the three people involved. All three will grow stronger.'

77. *Important details*

When people are asked to name the most amazing experiences of their lives the birth of their children usually features at the top of the list.

Jack and Anna had finished a meal and were in the kitchen. They surveyed the carnage of dirty pots and plates scattered around the work surfaces and realised the mess wouldn't clear itself. Jack turned to Anna, looking every bit eight and a half months pregnant, and said, 'Don't worry about the kitchen, I'll tidy it, but before I do let's just go in the other room and chill for a bit.'

Anna gave him a look and said, 'I'd like to but I can't relax if the kitchen is a mess. Either tidy it now, or I'll do it then join you for a relax.'

This was a recurring difference between Jack and Anna and it had played itself out many times before, and was destined to be replayed many times in the future. Couples are often attracted to each other's differences but then make the mistake of trying to change their partner to *their own right way*, which doesn't happen. Strong couples recognise and accept their differences and find ways to get along. In the future Jack would learn that even when he tidied the kitchen Anna would then have to finish it off properly. However, tonight was the night their first child was born.

At the sink, while Anna rinsed correctly and Jack dried incorrectly, she went into labour. A few hours later (ten) at the hospital Anna delivered a beautiful girl with a lick of cute black hair and a little red face. As Jack held her for the first time, wrapped carefully in blankets, he felt different. Inside this experience, for a moment, he glimpsed the real meaning and magnificence of life and of love.

We are part of the line, he thought to himself, each life a blink and an eternity. Jack saw the beauty and magic of the whole universe in the face of his daughter. And at that moment he remembered the Grey Lady stories his grandad had told years earlier. He pictured the vulnerable yet determined little chick he saw in the nest all those years ago while walking with Grandad. He had become more of an adult. He was now responsible for nurturing the perfect little girl he held in his arms. Her four tiny fingers wrapped around the forefinger he'd used to stroke her chin for the first time. He knew he would protect, prepare and promote her using the diamond strong bond that linked heart to heart from one generation to the next. He didn't mind whether she would grow up to wash up like her Mum or her Dad.

78. *Walking with cowboys*

Jack was watching a Harry Potter film with Grandad and heard Dumbledore say to Harry: 'It's not our abilities that show us who we really are; it's our choices.'

Jack asked his grandad which films he enjoyed watching the most. He thought he already knew the answer but wanted to explore a thought he'd had. Grandad did not hesitate to provide the answer Jack expected: Westerns. Grandad especially liked John Wayne and Clint Eastwood films. Jack asked why he liked these best.

'I like loads of things about them. The stories are good, they're about someone righting wrongs, sticking up for the weak, a hero that is honest, straightforward, brave and determined. The characters do the right thing. They're set in communities. Also the country. It's so big and just waiting to be explored.'

Jack then shared some of his grandad's wisdom from a few years earlier. Grandad had suggested to Jack that if we want to see inside of ourselves we could do so best by identifying what we admire in those we most respect. The values and actions of our role models and heroes are usually the values and actions that will serve us well in our own journey.

79. A new Sunday tea

Jack and Anna had a go at preparing a traditional Sunday tea and although they couldn't quite recreate the atmosphere and food from their memories they did have some great days. Rosy came over with her partner, their son Jason, and also brought Grandad. Later Jack, Anna and their daughter Lilla would take Grandad home via the allotment. The children's adoration of their great-grandad was reciprocated. He taught the children games and they loved it.

A favourite card game was My Lives. Each suit represented a super-power within us – hearts: love and support from friends, family and all the people we meet; diamonds: wealth, fame and fortune; clubs: good luck, fortune and career success; and spades: ability to over-come setbacks and determination.

Grandad challenged the children to imagine how their lives would turn out. They'd choose two cards and these would represent their age in this game. Today Jack chose a seven of clubs and five of hearts. He had to imagine how his life would be aged seventy-five with the cards of boundless love (hearts) and career success (clubs). Jack con-cluded he'd have been a fantastic teacher helping thousands of chil-dren in the North-East mine their brilliance. The combination of the cards and the children's imaginations created some amazing future lives for all of them to try on and describe.

80. *Looking for the magic inside the familiar*

Grandad was babysitting Lilla. She was excited because of a game she had played at nursery. She said she'd like to teach her grandad something. She brought over a piece of A4 paper and handed it to him. She explained that it was an amazing thing but the magic was hidden because we see it every day: 'When the sheet is folded in half it's exactly the same shape!'

She demonstrated how the length to width proportions were identical. 'This happens if you fold it again and again. Isn't that clever, Grandad?'

'Yes it is. Why is it like that?' he asked.

'It's so printers in the olden days could print the same page in different sizes without having to lay out a new page. Our teacher said there is magic like this in all of us, we just don't notice it.'

81. Expert or donkey?

Grandad was spending a few days with Jack and Anna. The house was a mess while their kitchen was being extended and refitted. Grandad and Lilla went off to the local park to escape the chaos. The builders had an impressive set of qualifications and tools. Grandad thought he wouldn't have trusted them to build a pigeon cree never mind a kitchen.

Lilla thought Grandad's mind was wandering because he was not pushing the swing properly.

'Higher, I want to go higher,' she bellowed through a smile and giggle. Next it was the slide and then the roundabout.

'You don't like the builders do you, Grandad?'

'It's not that, it's just I don't think they're doing a good job.'

'But they've got a brochure that says how good they are and very expensive tools.'

'You're a very perceptive girl, Lilla, so I'd like to share a saying I once heard: A donkey carrying a load of holy books is still a donkey.'

82. Values

Lilla told Jack she'd been learning about values at school. Today had been her turn to choose a value from a box. The teacher had made a Pandora's box but it contained only positive values that the children all agreed to spread around their world. Lilla picked out respect.

'Miss Dawson asked us who we respected most and I said you, Dad, because you're a teacher and that's the most important job in the world. She said we should ask that person who they respect most as a way to learn what respect means to different people. I'm supposed to ask you what you learned from that person.'

'I respected my grandad most. I learned to respect myself from Grandad. And become the kind of person I could respect. He was a great teacher but he never taught in a school. He once told me to be a learner and a teacher. You can't have one without the other. You've been my teacher, Lilla.'

'How?'

'When you were a toddler and you'd get out of the car at the park you'd stop and say "Wow!" at the trees, the puddles, squirrels scampering across the path, and loads of things. Toddlers are great at seeing the beauty and magic around them. They teach their parents because they've forgotten. Feeding the ducks was hilarious. You'd eat half the bread and throw half in the water. You once asked me what bread would taste like for a duck, which was brilliant. We had to think like ducks. You were a great teacher that day, Lilla. People who respect each other can be learners and teachers. Some people don't respect others and assume they are better than others. Other people don't respect themselves and assume others are better than they are. That's why I think respect is important. What do you think respect is about?'

83. *High standards*

Jack's neighbour Robin was renowned for being a 'character'. This is usually code for stubborn, awkward and difficult. He called a spade a spade. Most of the neighbours didn't appreciate him.

Robin was retired. He had trained plumbers. He had been made redundant around twenty years ago and told Jack the apprentices would have been so pleased he'd been made redundant they'd have had a party. Jack asked why he thought that way. Robin explained that there were four trainers and he was the toughest. Each year the standards required to pass the course were lowered by the certificating organisation but Robin ignored the instructions. He thought they should work to the same high standards he had always taught.

A few years ago Robin had some trouble with his modern boiler and couldn't fix it himself. He called a plumber to discuss the problem. After a few minutes the plumber revealed he knew who Robin was because many years ago he'd been trained by him. He took the opportunity to thank Robin for the high quality of instruction he delivered. He was sure this was why he had been able to establish a successful business. He said to Robin that he'd come round immediately and take on any job for free as he hadn't thanked Robin at the time because he didn't then appreciate the importance of the highest standards.

84. *Lost in IKEA*

Lilla awoke in the early hours following a nightmare. She got into her parents' bed and settled down. In her nightmare she said she had been trapped in IKEA. Jack felt this was less a nightmare and more a fifty-fifty chance you took on every visit. He was convinced the reason they have two cafes is to provide sustenance to any shoppers trapped inside overnight. Explorers like Ray Mears and Bear Grylls could train for their more arduous adventures by visiting IKEA.

At breakfast the next day Lilla asked why we have dreams. It's generally fantastic when children ask for information and advice from their parents. It's one of the things most parents look forward to as soon as they discover they're expecting. If only they wouldn't ask when you have five minutes to do ten minutes of chores before you leave for work.

'I remember my grandad's answer when I asked him that question around twenty years ago. It's because there are two directions in which our minds can travel, reality or imagination. We need to practice and develop in both directions and dreaming is a great place to use our imagination. We can daydream as well as nightdream. Sometimes the answers to problems are not available to us in the real world so our brain creates or invents. When we wake up we can then test out these ideas in the real world; the world where there are buses, sandwiches and forests. Good ideas have to be explored in both worlds. Most people just spend their time in one of these places. That's a waste. I've no idea why you were dreaming of being trapped in IKEA though. Tell me what you think on the way to school.'

85. Blackberrying

The first Sunday in September was so mild that a stroll was the ideal way to start the afternoon. This turned into a family blackberry picking walk near Grandad's allotment so various plastic containers were gathered into Jack's bag in anticipation of the treasure ahead. The warm sun complemented the gentle breeze, enough to encourage a few straw-coloured leaves from their branches. The route of the walk was familiar but some of the landmarks were novel. The field that had showcased the one-eyed horse was now a cul-de-sac of six executive-style homes. The field that staged triumphant bonfires was now a supermarket. Thankfully, the wood remained and the children toddled ahead slowly enough to enjoy the richness of activity around them. The children and Grandad enjoyed a similar optimum pace which meant each new type of tree or land feature was appreciated.

Grandad found a golf ball that he gave to Jason to throw back over the wall onto the golf course, while Lilla was distracted by the glimpse of a squirrel scampering up a huge tree trunk. They paused by the tree to guess at its age. The adults' pace had been hurried and busy but they had now succumbed to the slower pace of the rest of the group. Adults generally need very old or very young people around to slow them down to a more measured speed. The journey was not wasted. The blackberry hedges that criss-crossed along a section of ancient holly trees bore plenty of fruit to fill the containers they'd brought along. For half an hour they picked out the best berries available until their tubs were full and could be returned to Jack's backpack.

'Why are the branches prickly?' asked Lilla.

'The plant wants to give you something nice and sweet to eat but in return it wants to stop you taking too many berries. Then the seeds are more likely to be spread across the wood so more new bushes can grow. This is the way things work in nature, Lilla. There is a balance.'

When they returned home the children helped to make blackberry and apple pie which later everybody demolished with custard.

86. *Karate lessons*

Jack and Lilla were returning from a karate training session. Tonight they'd learned to aim past the target of their punch to generate more power. They'd also learned to rotate their hand slowly as they did so to minimise injury to the hand. They'd talked about this in the car and decided it was a good principle for other areas of life too. They were walking from the car to their front door.

It was cold and as they were wearing their karate outfits they wanted to slip in quickly and without being noticed. It was wishful thinking as Peter, the elderly neighbour from the house directly opposite, swooped in. He always seemed to pick the worst time to share his news. He proceeded to tell Jack about his latest test results. Peter was losing his eyesight and had nasty arthritis in his hands. Peter spent around fifteen minutes telling Jack and Lilla what he couldn't do any more.

Lilla interrupted and asked: 'What *can* you still do?' This stopped Peter in his tracks and he made his excuses and left. Lilla asked if she had been rude and Jack said, 'No, I think you're right. Doing what you can do is better than talking about what you can't do.'

87. Driving home

While driving home from a family day out Lilla looked out of the window and saw two women walking their dogs, unaware at this point that they would cross in the middle of the street. The first lady was tall and wearing a black beret. She was sauntering along slowly with her dog on a short lead, head down, unaware of the pretty gardens she passed. The other lady, who was smaller, had her dog on a longer lead and was marching quickly, perhaps she was singing a song in her head, while swinging a small plastic bag in front and behind her in the style of a windmill. Lilla realised the item she was swinging was almost certainly dog mess.

By now Grandad, sitting in the back with Lilla, had noticed what was happening. The two women were just about to pass each other.

'Imagine if the bag of dog mess split, Grandad, and it went on the little woman,' said Lilla.

'It looks like the little woman thinks it already has,' replied Grandad.

88. *Angel of the North*

Grandad had been saying to Jack that he'd like to visit the *Angel of the North* for a while. When it first appeared, Antony Gormley's prominent sculpture divided opinion. Some thought the money should have been spent on hospitals or schools and others saw it as a symbol of the renaissance of a North-East emerging into a new stage of its history. They parked in the slip road near to the statue and walked towards the imposing figure. Jack asked if Einstein had ever visited the allotment.

'He meant to but he got lost on the way. He ended up in Sacriston. It helped him to clarify his thoughts on parallel universes but meant he didn't get to see the ferrets.'

There was a strong blustery breeze whipping across the field which brought water to the eyes. Jack asked Grandad what he thought of the Angel as they approached the rusty curves of its legs. They were the only people there and they both touched the cold metal.

Angel of the North

'It's brilliant this isn't it, Jack? Look at the way the wings are angled in, it's like we're being embraced.'

'So you're not one those that think it's a waste of money?'

'No, that's just people not liking anything new. After ten years they'd complain if it was taken down. No, the North-East is changing, Jack. I was around just as one era ended – coal mining. You're around for a new one starting. I only worked in the pit for a year. Then me and the pit ponies were made redundant together. They were well looked after, the ponies. My grandad had died in the pit. A spark ignited and mixed with the coal dust. It blasted up the tunnel with such force and speed that he was blown out of his boots and the laces didn't even break, according to my Mum. I was relieved I wasn't going to go the same way and then did national service, travelled and had some amazing times.'

A few more people arrived just as they were leaving. They were a couple well wrapped-up against the elements. They exchanged smiles as they passed each other.

'I caught the travel bug after that and went off to sea with the merchant navy. We can never tell what's round the corner. This Angel will be around for a long time and we've no idea what changes she's going to see. Just make sure you're ready, Jack.'

Jack asked Grandad what he meant by 'ready'.

'Don't worry, you're ready. You're a learner and a teacher. I think you're a lot like this Angel, Jack.'

Jack was going to say he thought Grandad was like the Angel.

89. *Like or love*

Jack asked Lilla to turn off the TV because she wasn't particularly interested in the programme she was watching. She replied with the kind of disdain that implied she'd been requested to cut off her own arm rather than simply turn off the television.

A couple of minutes later Lilla asked her Dad if she should believe her teacher, who had said that if they worked hard at school they'd get good grades and find a job they'd like.

'Is that true, Dad?'

'Does studying get you a job you like? Well, I remember a friend of mine at university, Stuart, who loved two things in life: snorkelling and saving the planet. When he talked about them his eyes opened a little further than normal and his voice tone rose and quickened. He liked lots of other things: girls, beer, football, cricket and studying. For a research placement he arranged to go to a Caribbean island to study a coral reef to see if he could discover any environmental pressures affecting it. He loved it so much that he didn't come back to finish his degree.

'I went out to see him a couple of years after I'd finished my own degree. He had a successful business taking groups of tourists out snorkelling. Afterwards he would describe the reef and what could be done to protect it and the local environment in general. Some of the locals were famous people who owned property near the reef and they'd paid the government to protect it. The owners had been snorkelling with Stuart and his enthusiasm had been contagious. While I was there I noticed his eyes were even brighter and his speech even quicker than I remembered. I went snorkelling with him and it was amazing. When your body is under the water you do feel like you're in a different world. It's quiet and slow, everything moves gracefully and you see how beautiful the world is. The fish seem to glow, their colours are so rich. You wonder if you're on a different planet and then realise how precious this one is.

'He was engaged to a local girl. He was really happy. We did all of the things we liked as students. We talked about football and cricket and drank a little beer.

'Studying for good grades might have got Stuart a job he liked but instead he went for what he loved. Surely that's what we should be aiming for? Don't settle for what you like Lilla, discover what you love. That's why I'm switching the TV off now.'

90. *Word power*

Lilla was struggling with a piece of homework. The topic was unfamiliar words. Lilla said out loud *fecundity* three times as if this would help the meaning of the word leap from brain to mouth to pen. Jack intervened to prevent inadvertent yet inevitable swearing. Jack described fecundity as best he could. He described it as the number of babies an animal or plant produces. A spider might produce three hundred offspring whereas a human usually produces one at a time. The spider is more fecund. The number of babies produced normally depends on the survival rate. If only one in three hundred spiders is likely to survive then the end result will be similar for human and spider.

The next word was *alchemy*. Lilla had looked this up and understood what it meant but was looking for a quick definition as *Dr Who* was about to start. They settled on 'an ancient practice of trying to turn common metals into gold'.

Soon Jack and Lilla were watching *Dr Who*, 'The Shakespeare Code' episode. The power and magic within words is eloquently described by the Doctor as he breathlessly reminds us that the right combination of numbers can split the atom and there is an even more powerful magic within all of us, stirred by the right combination of words. When the right words pass from teacher to learner they can untether dormant brilliance. Words are the most fecund alchemy; exploding human potential, like a brilliant white star shattering light in all directions to fill a universe.

91. Fight club

Jack wanted to watch the film *Fight Club* with his wife Anna. It had been recommended by Grandad. She was not a fan of violence in films but he'd promised her he'd been told it was an excellent film and that the fighting was more metaphor than central to the plot. It was not a *Rocky* film. She'd watched a bit of the film but the metaphor was a tad too real for her taste. She later asked for a summary of the film. Rather than try a Jonathan Ross-style review he described one scene.

'The main character delivered random acts of killing. Hold on, he didn't kill the individual, he killed their sloth, their inertia, in order to reignite their ambition. He would pretend he was going to kill someone. Before doing so he asked what their dream was before they let mundane concerns consume their life. Once they revealed their dream in a terrified and heightened state of awareness he made the person promise to have the life they dreamed of, otherwise he'd find them and kill them. This motivated them to go and live their best life.'

Anna was a careers adviser and her methods of motivation were far less dramatic. This was, of course, his assumption as he'd never seen his wife at work.

92. *Switching it off and on*

'Have you tried switching it off and on again?'

Jack would like to say 'yes' to the polite if slightly patronising voice on the other end of the telephone because when we've gone to the bother of identifying a problem and sought professional help we want our problem to be worthy of our conscious effort.

We'd like our problem to be dissected and solved with the dedication, skill and rigour of Inspector Morse, who forages for two TV hours, meticulously piecing together a myriad of clues, before laying out his conclusions with a perfect blend of modesty and satisfaction. Like a grandad gently slotting the last piece of a troublesome jigsaw into place before standing back to first pause then admire his craftsmanship. We want our professionals to do the same.

We want to be congratulated for having such complex and difficult-to-solve problems, the likes of which they rarely see, hoping they'll write a thesis on our case or perhaps invent and name a new condition after us.

'No,' said Jack to the IT helpline assistant, 'I haven't switched it off and on again.'

'That's fine, I'll wait on the line while you do and we'll see if that works, OK?'

About forty-five seconds later he returned, crestfallen, to inform the adviser that her advice had worked. Apparently this works 90 per cent of the time.

'Thanks,' Jack offered meekly, trying to mask the disappointment in his voice.

93. *Walking with the Stars*

Jack knew his grandad would die one day. He'd always pushed this thought out in front of him further than his outstretched arms could reach. When it happened he kept the thought out there and also pushed away the love he felt for his grandad so it would not swallow him up and burn him away. Although this prevented the pain and tears it made everything seem unreal and in slow motion for a while. He wanted to pull in the love and warmth but was scared he'd drown in the intensity of the emotion. Too much of him was tied and twined to his grandad to know exactly where one started and the other finished. In the daze after the funeral he often thought he saw his grandad, only for the jolt of reality to reveal a stranger. He hadn't been to the allotment for about six months. Once his grandad's illness confined him indoors Jack felt it would be wrong for him to go there. It would be like trespass.

Jack walked to the allotment and he knew it would be the last time he made the walk that he'd made hundreds of times before. The plot would pass to someone else tomorrow so this was his last chance. He nearly didn't come but was pleased he did. He noticed everything as he walked up the steps again. Like someone taking a last look at a view on holiday, drinking it all in. He lifted the rope which hung over the gatepost and entered. He looked round and spent around twenty minutes remembering things he had done in each part of the allotment. It seemed much smaller. He thought of the Grey Lady and all the ghost stories that he and his grandad had shared so many years ago. He went over to the pigeon cree and sat in the seat. Although the pigeons had gone months ago he could still smell a hint of their presence. Or perhaps it was just his memory.

He looked down and saw a pair of his grandad's old boots. A busy silence. Jack picked up one of the boots and noticed a drop of water trickle onto the toecap. It had fallen from his cheek. The pain and love came in together, fast, intense and clawing. He noticed the heels of the boots. They were worn away in the corners, the same on both boots. He then cupped his own foot in his hand revealing the same pattern worn away on his own soles. At that moment he felt great. His grandad really was with him. They walked in the same way. Stars walking together.

Grandad's boots

Jack then looked up at the sky and although it was mid-afternoon he could see a big moon hanging in the cloudless blue. He thought there'd be a good chance of seeing stars tonight. They could look down at the allotment they'd visited. He thought of something he'd seen recently on television. Stephen Fry was praising Nelson Mandela at an event to mark his birthday. 'He is like our father, everyone's father. We love him because he shows us how great a human can be. He makes us wonder how good we can become as an individual and as a species. If we can all be just a fraction of the great man he is then the human race will prosper.'

As he sat he noticed a small fern leaf clinging onto life in a crevice within a rotting timber slat.

94. *The secret of a long life*

One of Jack's neighbours was Mrs Jones. She was a feisty and cheerful ninety-four-year-old and knew everyone. She looked after the rabbits and guinea pigs of the children living on the street when families went on holiday. She called the children by the names of their animals which they found amusing. Lilla was called Snowball after her rabbit. Jack once asked her for her secret to a long life.

'Each morning I wake up and hope the day will bring me three things: a new challenge or problem to solve; something beautiful to see, hear or touch; and the opportunity to talk to and connect with a person or animal. So far, each evening, when I review my day I am grateful that I always manage all three.'

Her approach to life contrasted with Peter and his wife who were in their late eighties. They were so organised. They proudly announced that they didn't buy each other gifts that could last more than a few months, because 'what would be the point?' Jack bought the couple a calendar last year which must have annoyed them as they'd now have to live for a whole year to get full use out of it. Rumour had it that Peter asked the local shop if he could buy a bag-for-life at a discounted price as he'd already had most of his life. They were always prepared for the next season rather than enjoying the one they were in.

Curiously, they were the first in the street to clear up the garden ready for winter. The garden furniture was locked away in mid-August to protect it. Jack once dreamt he saw Peter halfway up a tree in the night desperately shaking off its autumn leaves so he could end his winter preparations. He thinks it was a dream. They lived out of synch with the rest of the neighbourhood, always ready for the months ahead.

95. *Leaving a vacuum*

Jack was aware that an addition to a family creates changes for everyone. Jack joked he was fourth in rank in his family – behind Anna, Lilla and Bounty. He was ahead of Lilla's rabbit, but he was disappointed and surprised to slip down the rankings behind a vacuum cleaner.

He arrived home and was met at the door by an excited Anna. 'Quick, come in, I've got something amazing to show you.'

Jack was rarely ushered into the house with such gusto. Surely he was about to hear some incredible news. He was pushed into the living room and asked to sit down and close his eyes. He liked this game and sat in anticipation with his eyes squeezed tightly shut.

'You can open them now,' announced Anna.

His eyes focused revealing Anna standing with a new vacuum cleaner and a smile of pride that filled the room. To make up for the disappointment she could see in his face Anna proceeded to offer a demonstration. During the next fifteen minutes he sat as Anna role-played the various features and benefits of her new purchase. Wow, it can suck up right up to the skirting board. She even named it Trevor! Wow, it can swivel, and then Jack's mind began to wander. He noticed a familiar look on Anna's face and realised it was the blissful look she used to wear when they were first in love. Oh no, he thought to himself, she loves the vacuum cleaner more than me. He could accept being a lower rank than Lilla and Bounty but surely not behind something bought from Currys. He now knew how Snowball the rabbit felt.

Later that evening he thought he'd play with Trevor as a way to bond and lance any festering resentment and jealously. He was soon won over by Trevor's handsome features. Wow, he purred in a smooth, soothing tone reminiscent of Tom Jones and he did swivel with the elegance of a dancer from *Strictly*. The best feature of all was a lever which, when caressed gently with a socked foot, retracted the cord back into the chassis of the cleaning cylinder. Jack unwound it several times so that he could perfect his technique. After ten minutes he could control the speed of retraction with the precision of a keen young surgeon.

Barely a month later and Trevor was a pernicious pariah. While Jack had demonstrated his cord control, an over-zealous retraction had flung the cord with ferocity into the air and with a thud it hit Lilla on the head. Although no permanent damage was done to daughter or Trevor, Lilla had, probably reasonably, developed a phobia for vacuum cleaners and men named Trevor that would endure for years. In a similar repeat incident Jack accidently whipped in the plug via Anna's ankle. Even two hundred and fifty quid from *You've Been Framed* would not have made the bruises heal more quickly. Even Bounty now left the room if Trevor was brought into it.

96. *Sign of the times*

Jack and Lilla enjoyed watching the adverts between TV programmes. Jack thought they were a great way to understand language, persuasion and influence. They'd noticed that the more boring the product the more exciting the advert. Beauty products were a particular favourite. They often depicted serious looking people in white lab coats searching for ways to combat the horrors of ageing or the disaster of unshiny hair. They were currently enjoying 'the seven signs of ageing' advert. The ad focused on the face and listed wrinkles, blotchiness, age spots and so forth. Jack's friend Steve, a GP, had highlighted far worse signs of ageing including increased risk of heart attacks, strokes, falls and dementia. These made a few wrinkles seem far less scary. They continued the list game they'd started with Grandad.

The Star family's signs of ageing: choosing clothes for comfort or convenience over style (especially ties), climbing slowly out of (or slipping slowly into) chairs with a sigh of contented achievement, queuing more often, thinking about returning home even before you get to where you're going, saying a room is cold if it's not as hot as an oven on full blast and walking into a room and forgetting why.

The game had started a few years earlier. A five-year-old Lilla had been frightened by an advert announcing a cream that could make you look ten years younger. She asked Grandad if she applied the cream would she disappear out of existence or just become invisible. Grandad's response was to ridicule adverts by exposing the tricks they used. It became a game starting with the question, 'What is the advert really asking us to believe?'

97. *Vote Ant and Dec*

Lilla asked if she could vote for Ant and Dec as the family settled down to watch an awards ceremony. First they tried to remember the phone number they needed to ring but as they'd been watching television for more than an hour their brains had gone into 'hibernate mode'. Finding a pen and a piece of paper to record the number proved the best solution, forcing the family reluctantly from their soporific lethargy.

An hour in front of the TV and even urinating becomes a major hassle. What will become of us after a further three million years of evolution? thought Jack. Lilla cast her vote and returned to her seat.

'You know I've met Ant and Dec,' improvised Jack.

'Daaad, I'm watching this!' came the reply.

Jack ignored Lilla as he warmed to his theme: 'Yes, they're nice lads. We're in the same walking club, Lilla. They insist on walking together – mind you it has to be Ant to the left and Dec to the right. Even when they're climbing steep hills. They've told me some stories, Lilla.'

Jack was unaware that he'd just started the game with Lilla he'd shared with his grandad. Would Lilla also wear down the corners of her shoes?

98. *Grandad's wild weekend with Madonna*

This story has been removed following legal advice.

Part III
Interpreting the Stories

And, in the end, the love you take
Is equal to the love you make.

'The End', *The Beatles*

Possible interpretations and questions to accompany the stories

Some of the major themes of each story are highlighted in this section. If you're a fan of Dan Brown, Eddie Shoestring, Miss Marple and so on, and would rather piece together all of the clues yourself, then I admire your tenacity and work ethic and suggest you skip this bit.

If, on the other hand, you're more of a Barry Scott (Cillit Bang) or 'it does exactly what it says on the tin' kind of person then this section will offer reassurance and starting points with interpretations for the stories. Themes for each story are highlighted. Did you spot these? You could add a few of your own. There are also questions which can be used to generate discussion in groups or pondered individually.

1. *Swapping allotments*

- Our attitude affects both our journey and our destination.

- A positive outlook tends to lead to a positive outcome.

- Look for potential.

- Make the best of what you have.

QUESTION

What have you desired only to be disappointed once you owned it (toys, clothes, etc.)?

2. Birds that flock together learn together

- Communities are stronger than individuals.

- The world is connected and so is all of its life and all living things.

- Look at the world to understand it

QUESTION

When have you achieved more using teamwork rather than doing everything by yourself?

3. Who is your favourite?

- Ask yourself good questions if you want good answers.

- It's easy to convince ourselves based on flimsy evidence.

- Rather than thinking 'best' or 'favourite' look for the beauty in things.

QUESTION

Have you ever wasted time and energy wanting to be better than someone else rather than being *your* best?

4. Blowing up balloons

- Keep it as simple as it can be.

- Apply what you learn in the real world.

- When asked to blow up balloons avoid the long straight ones.

QUESTION

What things have you learned by observing others?

5. *Paper knickers*

- Focus on the direction of travel.

- We have a choice over what and how we remember.

- Laugh more.

QUESTIONS

What funny stories can you remember from your childhood? Do other people find these funny when you share the story?

6. *A sting*

- Nature is not benevolent (it only appears to be good or bad when we decide to be observer or judge).

- Look for the positive in things.

- Little things make big things.

- If you have a choice ask for cotton pants.

QUESTION

Can you think of things that have happened to you that at the time seemed bad but turned out well in the longer run?

7. *Dragonfly, frogs and toads*

- Find a niche.

- Then go and find some more because one is usually where endangered species live.

- Don't take people at face value.

- Don't swallow toads!

QUESTIONS

What are your comfort zones? How often do you move away from these?

8. *Gandhi visits the allotment*

- Strength comes in many forms (community, family and even a hippy bloke in a gown and sandals).

QUESTION

What are your strengths?

9. *Barking (1)*

- Some people complain about others to cover their complaints about themselves.

- The mood we pass on to others is usually the mood that is returned to us.

QUESTIONS

Do you ever talk negatively about some people to try to impress others? Do you think this works?

10. Barking (2)

- What we focus on we become.

- Choose love not aggression.

- People can and do change.

QUESTIONS

Can you think of times when you were kind to someone? How did that make you feel?

11. Gooseberry fools

- Listen to advice.

- Don't be greedy.

- Eat more than two kilogrammes of gooseberries in one sitting and you, your belly and your bottom will regret it.

QUESTIONS

What's the best advice you've been given? What's the best advice you've given to someone else? Do people usually take advice or ignore it?

12. *Inside out*

- Outer appearance and inner worth can be confused.

- Inner strength is needed and can be nurtured.

- Sometimes we are not ready to learn useful things.

QUESTION

To what extent do you judge people by their outer appearance?

13. *Outside in*

- If someone is not ready for advice we can try again later.

- Inner qualities cannot be judged by outer appearance.

QUESTION

What are the best ways to assess people?

14. *Hairstyle*

- Optimism is more useful than pessimism.

- Every situation offers opportunity.

- Do not be obsessed with how we look.

QUESTION

Why are people judged by how they look?

15. *Walking with Freddie Mercury*

- We can change someone's mood by distracting them, in this case using humour.

- We all wear masks to hide or reveal our true selves.

- The fun is finding out what's inside.

QUESTION

What masks do you wear and for what purpose?

16. *Too small to make a difference*

- We can all make a difference.

- We create our own reactions to information.

- Our moods motivate us to act or not.

QUESTION

When have you made a difference?

Source: Stephen Fry, John Lloyd and John Mitchinson, *QI: The Book of General Ignorance*, Faber and Faber, 2006.

17. *Mosquito nets*

- We can make a bigger difference when we learn how to influence others.

- When we do we are.

QUESTION

For what causes would you be motivated to do something?

18. *Not carrots and sticks*

- We can motivate ourselves by harnessing the energy of our own moods.

- We can motivate others by harnessing the energy of our own moods.

- We can motivate others by harnessing the energy of their moods.

QUESTION

How do you influence others?

19. *Billie Jean King*

- Successful people do not treat experiences as failures because they ask, 'What can I learn and how can I apply this learning?' This is a characteristic shared by all successful people in sport, the arts, business and parenting.

- Collecting feedback so we can improve our performance or skill is more useful than labelling ourselves as a failure.

QUESTIONS

In which situations do you give up? In which situations do you not give up?

20. *Negative or positive thoughts?*

- People are motivated in the short term through external fear/ threats but in the long term through positive internal goals.

- We're all scared of something (spiders, public speaking and death are the top three).

- Do not assume you know what people are thinking or what will or will not motivate them. And if it's appropriate, ask them to tell you what it is that motivates them. It is much quicker, accurate and polite this way round.

QUESTIONS

When do you assume you know what someone is thinking? Are you always accurate? What are the best ways to know what someone is thinking?

21. *Curiosity*

- Curiosity leads to action which leads to discovery and each discovery can tell us something useful.

- It's better to state instructions positively by suggesting people behave in the way you would like them to.

- It's also a good idea to not tell them.

QUESTION

When are you most curious?

22. *The Beatles at the allotment*

- Love is ultimately all we have and thankfully it is usually enough.

- There is much wisdom in pop songs.

QUESTION

What is the best wisdom you have found in a song?

23. *A light buffet*

- Only when we experience life can we taste the best of the world but we risk tasting the worst of the world too.

- Some people are on a very restrictive diet.

- We all remember events differently.

QUESTION

Ask someone how they remember an event you both attended and compare it to how you remember the event. Are there differences?

24. *The white horse*

- Our actions speak louder than our words.

- This applies to the words that we offer to others but also to the words we repeat inside our heads to ourselves.

- Don't try to fool your parents.

QUESTIONS

Have you ever tried to trick someone? What happened?

25. *Choices and abilities*

- Our choices (or lack of them) have a bigger impact than our abilities (or lack of them).

- Most people regret not doing more with their lives than regret the 'mistakes' they made.

- A cycle of live, learn, live, learn is not a bad way to move.

QUESTION

Who do you know that has made good choices (from your own family or famous people)?

> The chief danger in life is that you may take too many precautions.
>
> *Alfred Adler*

26. *Greasy Alan*

- Do not seek perfection; like trying to seek happiness, it's an illusion. We are wiser to direct our attention to where we are on the path, rather than the destination.

- 'Mistakes' are generally better understood with tears of laughter than tears of regret or embarrassment.

- Beware seeking perfection as it is only an idea from inside our own head, not an objective reality.

Can you think of examples where the anticipation of something was better than the thing itself? How can we know when something is good enough or decide whether we could do better?

27. *Present*

- Nurturing our imagination and creativity is a great gift to ourselves.

- Children are generally focused on the present.

QUESTION

Do you daydream? What about? When is it useful? When is it not useful?

28. *Walking with Paul Daniels*

- Is it better to play it safe or take risks?

- Developing our skills increases our chances of making good decisions.

QUESTION

When are you a risk-taker and when do you play it safe?

29. *What do big girls talk about?*

- Don't waste your time on loops of thought that take you in a negative direction.

- We think we'd like to be with the cool kids but close up they can look different.

QUESTIONS

Do you think negative thoughts about yourself? What impact does this have on you and those around you? What makes someone 'cool'? Can you decide you are cool or does the label have to be given to you by others?

30. Travelling

- The best experience is experience.

- Make the most of where you are.

- Learn from outside as well as inside yourself.

QUESTIONS

Where have you travelled? What impact has travel had on you?

(Note: The Llangollen International Musical Eisteddfod does indeed still run every year.)

31. Ghost story (1)

- Move forward positively in all the things you do and you will be rewarded.

QUESTIONS

Have you been told a ghost story? Why do we like to be scared?

32. Richie Benaud

- Seek to understand things by breaking them down into the important steps and removing the stuff that isn't important. This is not easy but it is very useful.

- It is not knowing what to do that is difficult; it is doing it, day after day after day that requires the best human qualities.

QUESTIONS

If you had to write down all the useful things you know on just one sheet of A4, what would you write? Which things can be improved with practice? Which things can practice not improve?

33. FA Cup final day

- If you let people down, acknowledge it to yourself and the other person. If you can put it right, do so.

QUESTION

Does saying sorry help?

34. Leek sleepover

- Protect what it is important to protect.

- We need imagination *and* reality, mind *and* body, to understand.

QUESTION

What are your best memories?

35. Ghost story (2)

- Fear motivates.

QUESTION

What are your greatest fears and how can you use this information to motivate yourself positively?

36. Bruce Forsyth

- Dancing together is better than dancing alone.

- Work hard and develop self-discipline to make the most of your skills.

QUESTIONS

Do you have skills you've worked hard to develop (eating, walking, doing up your shoelaces, a sport)? What are the most useful skills?

37. A focus of attention

- Sometimes we need to focus on what is happening inside our bodies and at other times what is happening on the outside. Choose the right one for the situation at hand.

- Sometimes it's both.

QUESTIONS

Where are you directing your attention now? In which situations do you direct your attention inside/outside of your body? Why does time seem to pass really quickly sometimes and really slowly at other times?

38. *Real education*

- To reveal the true value of people they must be nurtured not neutered.

- We need to feel loveable (or loved) and capable to learn.

QUESTIONS

When do you learn best? What have you learned that was easy? What have you found more difficult to learn? Why?

39. *Mountain climbing*

- Our attitude determines our altitude – literally in this story.

- Attitude is often more important than skill.

QUESTIONS

What is a good attitude? In which situations has your attitude been useful/not useful?

40. *Doing the right thing*

- If we help others they may help us.

- Be nice to people on your way up as you might meet them again on your way down.

QUESTIONS

Should we help others in expectation of receiving help in return? Why are some people more altruistic than others?

41. Alan Bennett's last meal

- People reveal far more than they think in the words they choose.

- If we listen carefully there is much we can learn from the words used.

QUESTIONS

Do you think about the questions people ask or do you focus on the answer you're going to give? What would happen if we all focused more on the questions?

42. Bounty

- We gain a bigger return using love than we do using fear.

- A great way to learn something is to teach it or experience it.

- Children can learn about responsibility, trust, love and friendship when they look after a pet (unless it's a fish that often seem to perish quickly).

- The dog as a blood donor helped other dogs. Remember we send out ripples from our own actions that can have a wider impact than we can predict.

QUESTIONS

What are the important emotions? How do you know? How did you learn about these?

43. Beer mats

- We can learn much from our peers.

- The more energy we generate the more energy is returned our way.

QUESTIONS

Why do people like collecting things (plates decorated with a kitten playing with a ball of wool, train numbers, stamps, etc.)? What have you learned from friends/family?

44. *Penalty shoot-out*

- Children learn by role-modelling.

QUESTIONS

Who are your role models? Ask yourself, 'What would they do?' when faced with challenges. You might welcome the insight provided.

45. *Walking with David Attenborough*

- Be aware of your inner and outer environments and apply the knowledge to learn about both.

- Being true to our own values brings greater reward than seeking material gain and status.

QUESTION

What are the biggest decisions you've made in your life so far?

46. *Walking through time*

- Contemplate your best future and begin to plan for it.

- We all have inner wisdom and resources to draw upon.

QUESTION

What is the best that could happen to you in your life? Consider the detail. Perhaps contemplate four or five ways in which you could have a fantastic life. Then plan for the one which most appeals to you.

47. Barking (3)

- Be wary of overprotecting those you care for.

- People and places can and do change.

QUESTION

Can you spot the challenges, risks and obstacles that may lie in front of you?

48. Successive approximations

- A plan is useful but always be flexible within a plan; the best progress is made by successive approximations.

QUESTION

Which people are best suited to advise and support you over the next few years?

49. Grandma's rugs

- A journey is better than a destination because it is on the journey that we experience life fully; a destination is an end.

- We understand things more after we do them ourselves rather than watch someone else do them.

QUESTIONS

Have there been endings and beginnings in your life to date? What is their relationship to each other? What impact have these had?

50. *Jack's favourite childhood toy*

- There are times in our lives when we achieve flow, nirvana (a heightened state of bliss), presence or enlightenment.

- We must recognise and enjoy these moments fully.

- If we strive for magic moments we will find more of them than if we wait for them.

QUESTION

What are your magic moments?

51. *Perception is reality*

- If we share a secret it may be spread around.

- People have many beliefs; understanding their beliefs is more useful than deciding whether their beliefs are right or wrong.

QUESTIONS

When have rumours influenced you? Have there been times when you've acted upon false information? What was the impact?

Source: Stephen Fry, John Lloyd and John Mitchinson, *QI: The Book of General Ignorance*, Faber and Faber, 2006.

52. *Your hardest day's work*

- When we truly test ourselves we truly understand ourselves.

- People usually report they are far stronger than they could have believed or imagined when faced with daunting challenges.

QUESTIONS

What have been the greatest challenges you've faced? What impact have these had on you? Which films have had a big impact on you?

Mr Quinn is a tribute to all great teachers but especially to John Taylor Gatto's book *Dumbing Us Down*.

53. *The Hoppings*

- Enjoy the journey; do not focus only on a destination.

- Choice requires options – without options we get stuck.

- Fortune tellers can predict the future accurately only when people choose to believe their predictions.

- When we feel nervous (or other negative moods) we say things we regret.

QUESTIONS

If you were to foretell your own fortune, based on what you know about yourself and the choices ahead, what would you predict? Have you made mistakes because you were nervous?

54. *Hatching time*

- As we grow and develop we benefit from a mentor sharing and enjoying our progress.

QUESTIONS

Have you seen something or someone change? How have you changed? Do you have a mentor?

55. *Building a pigeon cree*

- Knowing what we can't yet do is as useful as knowing what we can do.

- Being able to recognise these things is a powerful attribute.

QUESTIONS

Can you recognise things you can't yet do? What is the best thing to do about it?

56. *The Merlin factor*

- We're all unique with our own strengths and talents.

- Learn from those we most admire and a little of their magic will fall on us.

QUESTIONS

What have you been designed to do/be? When are you at your best? If you pulled a sword from a stone and then thought you could then do anything, what would you do? From which three people could you learn most?

57. Sunday tea

- Do things for the right reasons.

QUESTIONS

Do you know when you're doing something whether it's the right (or wrong) thing to do? Does everyone have this awareness? When have you done the right thing?

58. Tony Marbles

- We must learn from those we admire so we can be *our* best, not a copy of them.

- Aim to be our best, not to be better than someone else, otherwise either they or you lose.

- You often hear people say life is like sport but it isn't!

QUESTIONS

Why is life not like sport? What have you won or lost?

59. Victoria Beckham

- Moods spread so spread good moods.

- People are not always what you think they are.

QUESTION

When have you spread good moods around?

60. My very last trip to Billy the barber's

- Let people know what you're thinking because there are very few mind readers around. You'll avoid more than a bad haircut.

QUESTIONS

When do you speak up for yourself? What are the most important things you've learned in your life so far?

61. The rules of whistling

- There are times when our identity is not clear.

- We look for external rules when the more useful place to look is inside.

QUESTION

What are the rules of life?

62. Elvis and Marilyn

- We move in and out of many moods and we can all access very powerful moods. Be aware of your moods and notice that it is useful to have an on/off switch you can use.

- Even the most apparently confident people may not be so self-assured inside.

QUESTIONS

Are there parts of your life where you are more confident than in others? Why?

63. An interesting lift

- There are answers everywhere.

- Some of the most obvious (and best) answers are the most difficult to spot.

QUESTION

Why do you think the staff at the lift company missed the answer spotted by Jack?

64. Lisa

- At times of doubt it can be better to turn inside for answers than to seek it from others.

- The answers may not always be comfortable.

QUESTION

How have you changed as you've got older?

65. Jumble sale

- Timing is important.

- When we notice change around us, consider how it might affect us.

- Ensure you have choices when confronted with changing environments.

QUESTION

During change, when have you built walls and when have you built windmills?

66. *Bazza the coach*

- Doing something is not always better than doing nothing.

QUESTION

In what situations have you felt under pressure and done something even when you weren't sure it would help?

67. *Cigarettes and alcohol*

- We are guided by our values and beliefs; if these are good our choices will usually be good.

QUESTIONS

When have you been influenced by peer pressure against your better judgement? Did things turn out better or worse as a result?

68. *Cheek to cheek*

- When we live out our values and beliefs we are in balance with both the internal and external world; we resonate with the universe.

QUESTION

Have you had an amazing week when loads of good things have happened?

69. *Bonty night*

- Adults guide us and help us grow strong roots. The values they pass on then become our inner compass that we must learn to pay attention to. When we can do this for ourselves we become adults.

- Many people never become adults.

- Peer pressure is a strong force; it can protect us or it can lead us away from our own values and beliefs.

- We can easily fall into the trap of living in the past or the future. It is in the present where all the magic is found.

QUESTION

What changes have you noticed in society over the past few years?

70. *Answering Lisa*

- We have a choice over how we feel.

- We can choose to accept or reject feedback, praise or criticism.

QUESTION

For whom or what would you stand up?

71. *Rainbows*

- Enjoy the world as it really is and the people within it as they really are – not as something to be bent and twisted to a shape that suits your present needs.

QUESTIONS

Have you ever fully enjoyed the moment? Have you been awestruck by a natural phenomenon (sunset, mountain view, butterfly wing, autumn leaf, etc.)?

72. *A night at the club*

- Friendship and camaraderie are valuable.

- Being part of a tribe brings security but we can surrender our own beliefs and values in the process.

QUESTIONS

Which tribes/gangs (football team, religious group, etc.) do you belong to? What does membership provide? Are there good tribes/gangs we can join (blood donors)? What might be healthy and unhealthy examples of tribes/gangs?

73. *A holiday in Cyprus*

- Discover your passion and follow it.

- Live in the present and plan for the future, but not in too much detail.

QUESTIONS

Are money and happiness linked? Many people stay working in a job they don't like by thinking of enjoying their retirement. Is this a good idea?

74. Grandad's CV

- When we delude ourselves we obscure our truth.

- Remember, we are looking at the world through our eyes, ears and heart – not at the world as it actually is.

QUESTIONS

If we could see the world as it really is, what would we see? What path are you on?

75. Get knotted buns

- If we believe something strongly enough it can come true. This can be good or bad.

- Sometimes decisions are made easier by the events around us.

QUESTIONS

Have you ever told a lie, unwittingly, when you thought you were right and found that people believed you? Why can this happen?

76. Wedding day advice

- We want to help people we like and love.

- We can spread good or bad thoughts.

QUESTIONS

Do you agree with the advice given? Could you try it out for a week and notice the impact?

77. *Important details*

- We mature day by day.

- We are different and would do better to accept difference rather than try to make everyone think and behave in the way we like.

QUESTION

In what ways are you similar to and different from your family and friends?

78. *Walking with cowboys*

- The values we would most like to aspire to personally are those we admire in our heroes and role models.

QUESTIONS

Which types of films/TV programmes do you most enjoy? What do the main characters have in common? What can you learn about yourself from these shared qualities?

79. *A new Sunday tea*

- Daydreaming your best future plants the best seeds.

QUESTION

What happens when you try the card game described?

80. *Looking for the magic inside the familiar*

- Look for the positive inside ourselves and we'll find it.

- Look for the positive in others and we'll find it.

QUESTIONS

How well do you pay attention to the familiar? Try remembering a room in your house in detail. Write down how you see it then check how accurate you were. You can try this with people. Can you remember their hair colour, the way it's parted, ear shape, eye colour, favourite food, book and so on? The people we see every day can be strangers. The TV programme *Mr and Mrs* demonstrates that people married for many years often know surprisingly little about each other.

81. *Expert or donkey?*

- Be wary of those seeking to impose their wisdom on you.

- Look for experts that seek to remove confusion rather than generate it.

QUESTIONS

When you meet people, what impresses you? How long does it take for you to form an opinion about someone?

82. *Values*

- Live in and enjoy the present moment.

- Spread positive energy around the world to enhance it.

When was the last time you learned something? When was the last time you taught someone something?

83. *High standards*

- We don't appreciate the things we learn immediately.

- High standards tend to pay off over time.

QUESTIONS

Has someone (a teacher, parent, peer) ever pushed you further than you thought you could go and you succeeded? Can you believe in other people more than you believe in yourself?

84. *Lost in IKEA*

- To survive and flourish, in IKEA or in the rest of the world, we need to develop our imagination and understanding of the real world.

- A guide can help us ask ourselves more interesting questions but will not provide us with answers.

QUESTIONS

Have you ever felt lost? When you compare this feeling with a time you felt safe and certain, what are the differences?

85. *Blackberrying*

- There is a natural balance and pace.

- It is best to discover and appreciate this.

QUESTIONS

Are there times when you feel out of step with the pace around you (either everyone else is moving too quickly or too slowly)? Are there times you feel in balance with the pace you are going?

86. Karate lessons

- It is best to aim a little further, just beyond your target.

- There is nothing to be gained from concentrating on what we can't do.

QUESTIONS

When have you concentrated on doing what you can do? When have you concentrated on talking about what you can't do? What is the impact of these different approaches?

87. Driving home

- Our attitude causes our experiences, not the other way round.

QUESTION

Have you decided on whether you're going to have a good day or bad day before the experience and made it happen (a day out, a holiday, a party)?

88. Angel of the North

- Change is constant though the pace of change is quickening.

- Some people are better able to deal with change than others.

QUESTION

What is your attitude to change?

89. *Like or love*

- Choose activities that provide internal not external satisfaction (i.e. to be better than someone else) for real fulfilment.

QUESTIONS

Do you know what you love doing? Do you know what you like doing? What's the difference?

90. *Word power*

- Words are powerful; they move people to act for good or bad causes.

- The words we speak inside our own heads are the most powerful of all.

QUESTION

Can you create a powerful sentence? It could be something really positive about yourself or a friend.

91. *Fight club*

- Motivation wears many clothes.

- Many people never get around to having the life they'd like.

QUESTION

What will it take for you to have the life you really desire?

92. *Switching it off and on*

- We'd like to think our problems are big and complicated and special.

- Most of our problems are neither real nor really big.

- We all have an on/off switch.

QUESTIONS

Which problems do you create and grow inside your head? Are they really real? What does it feel like to just fire them off into the distance so they disappear?

93. *Walking with the Stars*

- We are connected to the people we love.

- We don't always notice or appreciate the positive ways in which those we love influence us and nudge us towards being our best.

QUESTION

Who do you love?

94. *The secret of a long life*

- Enjoy the present.

QUESTIONS

Are you enjoying the present? What will you be enjoying later today? Tomorrow?

95. *Leaving a vacuum*

- We can feel threatened by the arrival of new people into our family or community.

- Our popularity can rise and fall.

QUESTION

How have you been affected by new arrivals to a group in which you belong?

96. *Sign of the times*

- People try to influence us.

- It is useful to be aware of this and choose our own response.

- We often focus our thoughts on the least important things.

QUESTION

Which adverts (or people, books, teachers) have influenced you? This story is inspired by Steve McKevitt's marvellous book *Why the World is Full of Useless Things* (Cyan Books, 2006).

97. Vote Ant and Dec

- Many people say we become our parents (this thought is usually greeted with either horror or a resigned shrug of the shoulders).

QUESTION

What would you like to pass on to the generations that follow you?

98. Grandad's wild weekend with Madonna

- We have powerful imaginations.

- We all have stories to tell.

- The best answers are found within.

QUESTION

What do you think happened during this wild weekend?

NLP and the stories

Neurolinguistic programming (NLP) was developed around forty years ago by Richard Bandler and John Grinder. They studied successful therapists who had achieved great results with those people they sought to help. NLP has become a field in which successful people across many disciplines are studied. The idea is that we can all learn from the behaviours, attitudes and beliefs used by the best performers in any area of human endeavour.

For example, how do people learn best? The natural way children learn is to copy those around them through role play without fear of failure. Children learn really well this way. It is estimated they learn around ninety new words per day before their seventh birthday. Children may not learn *best*; research shows that adults have more effective and efficient strategies for learning specific tasks or information. But it's certainly true that children learn *easiest*, at least until they begin formal schooling and start worrying about mistakes. The NLP Learning State was developed by observing the ways children and adults really learn best. By copying their techniques we can all learn more effectively. The Learning State is described in my book *The Buzz* (Crown House Publishing, 2006).

The basic assumptions underlying NLP can be found in these stories. Richard Bandler asserts that stories are the best way to understand NLP and its applications. The assumptions are not proven but it's useful to behave *as if* they are true and notice the difference in the results you get.

Ten useful assumptions to hold

1. The ability to change the process by which we experience reality is usually more valuable than changing the content of our experience.

In his book *Man's Search for Meaning*, Victor Frankl describes his experiences inside a Nazi concentration camp with chilling honesty.

One of his many powerful observations was that a key reason why some people survived and others did not was in large part due to their attitude. The prisoners had little control in most areas of their life but they could control their attitude and the way they experienced reality. We can all choose our attitude.

Stories 5, 6, 7, 24, 37, 44, 57, 59 and 62.

2. The meaning of communication is the response you get.

The problem with communication is the illusion that it has been accomplished.

George Bernard Shaw

Rather than blaming people for not understanding us, we can achieve better results by noticing the response we get as we communicate. We can observe the non-verbal signals and other behaviours to check whether or not our message was received the way we wanted it to be. Most of us do this naturally when we communicate with babies. If they don't understand us we look for clues in their reaction to help us communicate more effectively the next time we try. We do not blame the baby for being *wrong*. We tend to be less forgiving with older children and adults. Indeed, a survey recently discovered that the parents of teenagers routinely criticise their children in 90 per cent of their communications rather than seeking clarity. If someone does not respond to us in the way we were hoping then it is more useful to change the way we communicate rather than label the other person as being resistant, stupid or awkward.

Stories 16, 17, 20, 33, 38, 51 and 60.

3. All human experiences are filtered through the five main senses (sight, hearing, touch, taste and smell).

For example, all of our memories are experienced using some or all of our five senses. Think of your best holiday and you'll probably picture the place where you stayed. You will recall the things you heard and remember how you felt as if you were there. Can you remember your first kiss? Most people can. They can usually remember what they were wearing, where they were, what was said just before and after and certainly how it felt. If you're thinking, 'So what!' then that's fine until you realise that by changing these words, pictures and feelings you can change your memories. As an illustration, think of someone you don't like and notice where you picture this person. Most people say just in front and slightly above their eyeline. If you now move this picture down and away from you the negative feelings you may have for this person usually diminish.

Stories 3, 12, 35, 39, 41 and 56.

4. The resources individuals need to effect change are already within them.

There is a joke in solution-focused therapy that when all else fails you can ask the client for the answer. Conversely, in NLP-based therapy it is the client who is usually asked first to identify potential answers or useful ways forward. In my experience this is far better than trying to come up with all the answers for the client. If you were driving around in an unfamiliar place, the best person to ask for directions is someone who knows the area well. Clients know themselves far better than their adviser and they are usually able to identify the best solutions to their perceived problem.

Stories 14, 15, 29, 32, 36 and 46.

5. The map is not the territory.

The maps we create inside our minds and bodies can be amazing works of imagination and skill. However, they are maps and not the reality. Most of our maps are useful to us but some may be unhelpful. Creating a new map is more effective than trying to change the rest (or some) of the world and the people within it to fit in with our notion of how they or the world should be.

Stories 1, 22, 30, 45, 47 and 53.

6. The positive worth of the individual is held constant, while the value and appropriateness of the behaviour is questioned.

This concept has become part of most areas of mainstream therapy and pre-dates NLP. For example, it is better to question the benefit of someone's behaviour rather than to suggest they are a bad person. It is more beneficial to seek an appropriate pattern of behaviour than to label someone as the problem.

Imagine we're in a cafe and we overhear two couples on either side of us talking as follows:

Girlfriend A to Boyfriend A: 'I don't appreciate that particular behaviour of yours (buying a motorbike without saying) but I do still love you.'

Girlfriend B to Boyfriend B: 'You haven't bought me flowers for ages so I know you're a selfish person.'

I don't know about you but I'd rather be in relationship A.

Stories 8, 9, 10, 13, 27 and 55.

7. There is a positive intent behind every behaviour, although the person may not be consciously aware of it.

Have you ever heard your inner voice saying something horrible to you? This self-talk can create powerful and enduring negative beliefs. Finding the positive intention behind the words can be a cathartic experience.

I've worked with many people carrying around negative beliefs, passed on, perhaps unwittingly, by parents, teachers or even friends. They hear a parent's voice in their head saying, 'You're stupid.' When asked, 'Why might your parents have said that?' the answer could be, 'Because they don't want me to make a fool of myself.' 'Why wouldn't they want you to make a fool of yourself?' 'Because they love me.' When people recover the positive intent behind the behaviour, it is like a weight being lifted, allowing them to listen to other, more useful internal dialogue.

Stories 18, 23, 34, 49, 52 and 61.

8. Successful communicators accept and use all communication and behaviour presented to them.

We give out a great deal of information about our thoughts and beliefs through our words, our tone of voice, our body language, our eye movements and our posture. If we are aware of all of these clues we can better understand ourselves and each other. A great way to develop our own communication skills is to observe characters in films, soaps or people being interviewed on TV. Imagine being that person. Inhabit their body posture, speech patterns, voice tone and accent and we often obtain great insights into their true character. Actors do this as part of their work and it is a great way for us all to develop our own empathy, sixth sense, emotional intelligence, female intuition or whatever you want to call it.

Stories 2, 4, 19, 25, 28, 31, 40, 48 and 54.

9. Feedback not failure – we can find useful learning from all of our behaviour.

This attitude is a common habit of successful people. It is not that they don't fail. It is that they do not consider experiences as pass or fail. They tend to ask themselves what they can learn from all experiences and think about how they can apply this learning in the future. As Richard Branson said: 'I've learned far more from my failures than I have from my successes.'

Stories 11, 21, 26, 42, 43, 50 and 58.

10. We function most effectively when our identity, values, beliefs, behaviour and environment are consistent (congruent).

He who has a why to live for can bear with almost any how.

Friedrich Nietzsche

The people we most admire tend to be those who appear to combine a strong sense of internally driven purpose with contentment, calm and a generosity of spirit. They appear utterly comfortable in their own skin. They seem to know their strengths and how best to apply these to make their life full and rich. Many theories and religions give a name to this state such as self-actualisation. This state is associated with charisma, which is explored fully in my book *The Little Book of Charisma* (Crown House Publishing).

Stories 61, 73, 78, 82, 89, 91 and 93.

Further reading

Andreas, S. *NLP: The New Technology of Achievement*, Nicholas Brealey, 1996.

Frankl, V. *Man's Search for Meaning*, Pocket Books, 2004.

Fry, S., Lloyd, J. and Mitchinson, J. *QI: The Book of General Ignorance*, Faber and Faber, 2006.

Gatto, J. T. *Dumbing Us Down*, New Society Publishers, 2006.

Hodgson, D. *The Buzz*, Crown House Publishing, 2006.

Hodgson, D. *The Little Book of Inspirational Teaching Activities*, Crown House Publishing, 2009.

Hodgson, D. *The Little Book of Charisma: Applying the Art and Science*, Crown House Publishing, 2010.

Huxley, A. *The Doors of Perception*, Vintage, 2004.

Lees, B. *No Place*, Lintons, 2004.

McKevitt, S. *Why the World is Full of Useless Things*, Cyan Books, 2006.

Owen, N. *The Magic of Metaphor: Stories for Teachers, Trainers and Thinkers*, Crown House Publishing, 2001.

Owen, N. *More Magic of Metaphor: Stories for Leaders, Influencers and Motivators*, Crown House Publishing, 2004.

Owen, N. *The Salmon of Knowledge: Stories for Work, Life, the Dark Shadow and OneSelf*, Crown House Publishing, 2009.

Pearson, H. *Racing Pigs and Giant Marrows*, Abacus Books, 1997.

Wenger, W. *The Einstein Factor*, Prima, 1996.